Stealth

STEVE FOWLER

Thought Leader Press

Stealth

In honor of those who teach me to see the world
through their eyes every day.

In honor of those who teach me to see the world
through their eyes every day.

A PERSONAL INVITATION

This book is a reflection of my own journey—a journey filled with lessons, insights, and moments of clarity that have shaped who I am today.

What you'll find here isn't meant to be definitive. It's an offering. Some ideas may align with your own thinking, sparking new insights. Others may challenge you, and that's where the real growth begins.

Take what speaks to you, leave what doesn't, and let these pages encourage you to look deeper and ask bigger questions.

This is not about answers—it's about possibility. My hope is that these reflections will not only resonate with you but also empower you to lead with greater intention and authenticity.

TABLE OF CONTENTS

INTRODUCTION

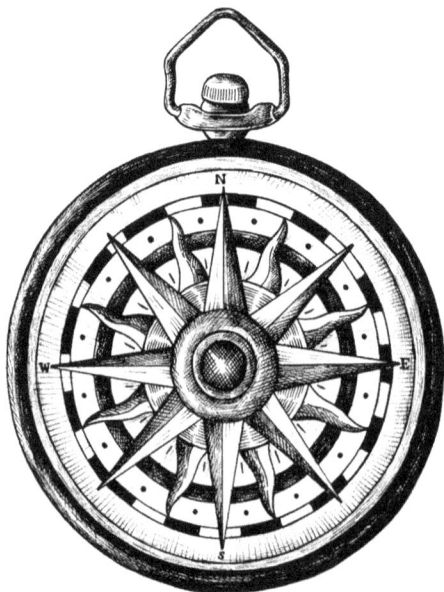

Most people have a childhood memory that gives them some solace and comfort, even bolstering their confidence.

Mine is my Batman costume. Growing up, I was a Batman fan. Later, when 'The Dark Knight' series came out, it completely resonated with me, teaching me to project myself more confidently by understanding who I was and the challenges I faced.

I still have challenges, and I am far from perfect. Perfection is elusive, but I love what I am learning about myself; this is what I hope this book is about.

I'm writing for those who feel like they are stuck and are looking for a way to grow and evolve.

This book is meant to help people gain more introspection and knowledge about themselves. It is for people chasing a mirage in a desert who realize they will not find any water.

It is for people who are searching for something new in themselves to improve, develop, and grow.

When it comes to growth, there is a convergence between our identities at work and those in our personal lives. Convergence is important to avoid having a dual personality.

I experienced the dual personalities between my work and home identities and saw how it negatively impacted me with my family, relatives, friends, and workplace.

I placed precedence on values that were affecting me negatively. I learned that I was enabling myself to go down certain paths where, at first, I was seeking to be accepted for who I am and focused too much on blending in.

I was associating with a group of people who knew nothing about me or my background. I sought an idealism that was not authentic and created more chaos in me than I had realized.

If you are seeking a change within yourself, this book might give you a set of ideas to help with that. I hope, more than that, it also grapples with the human condition and life struggles.

Oftentimes we allow others the power to create our reality, and that must be contested. This book is about checking yourself regarding what is real and what is a fallacy based on fears, biases, or beliefs.

I share my early experiences and vulnerabilities and then how I came to understand and prioritize myself rather than the figments or ideologies created by someone else.

I was chasing power and success and wanted to be someone like Bill Gates or Steve Jobs. I wanted their influential attributes that I did not fully understand or comprehend.

I was chasing a framework of influence rather than truly influencing from within.

I was chasing self-validation.

I was chasing an illusion of confidence.

I was chasing career advancements purely through bravado.

I had experiences, maturity, and competence; I was trying to chase success through negative attributes of extraordinary, false, and self-created opportunities.

During my career, I have even at times become what I would call an 'asshole' version of Steve. At some of those points, despite being a leader in my position, my behavior wasn't being rewarded any longer, and I was forced to stop and reflect as to why.

Listening to the feedback from the people who truly cared about me and wanted to see me be successful was game-changing. Whether they knew it or not, they were more than just career mentors, they were life mentors. They cared to show me care.

We are all aspirational to some degree, affected by our confidence or fears. Confidence can be exuded abnormally and extraordinarily because we are trying to parrot an industry leader or hero, but parroting has limits.

We all know the phrase, "Polly wants a cracker," but what does that mean? Does a parrot know what a cracker is? Does a parrot know how to reward itself for the parroting? No, it is simply repeating what it has been taught.

My epiphany came when I realized that my antics were no longer working. My experiences made clear that I needed to reset, seek help, and truly take advantage of the help.

I aspire to help people who are in similar situations like mine and who want to adapt and grow.

I certainly don't want to promise any specific goal toward individual growth, but I am more certain in my aspirations than I ever have been. I have more clarity, and that in itself is liberating.

We all tend to frame our aspirations, goals, achievements, sadness, or despair in a certain way because we want to make sense of it.

We want to rationalize our considerations, life events, and aspirations.

We ultimately create these compartmentalizations and rationalizations of various emotions, life experiences, or aspirations.

We create the experience and framework.

We have to get to a place where we can blow it up and reassemble ourselves, whenever and as often as we need to.

It has to be carefully managed; we can easily fall into traps like creating chaos for ourselves and subsequently have to reframe that chaos, creating a vicious cycle.

This book has provided more focus and clarity for me by understanding who I was and who I wanted to be.

I want to truly be me, more than having to be some idealized version of myself.

I need to understand myself and what I care about the most.

Writing this book has allowed me to care about myself, more than ever before. Caring about myself allows me to care about others in far more fluid ways than I had ever imagined.

I hope people will connect with me and talk about self-discovery, unleashing their potential, mastering their mind or mindset, having breakthroughs past their boundaries, and learning through life lessons.

I would love to share those thoughts and have others share theirs as well. Let's share life lessons and see if there are any parallels that we can draw from them together.

Embarking on this journey is akin to setting out on a road trip; discovering routes that lead to whatever form of success you're in pursuit of. It's an exploration of courage, steering through life's challenges with resolve. Along the way, this adventure cultivates and encourages dialogues that open doors to new possibilities.

The encouragement and advice that I share are opportunities. Read each chapter to realize your beginning, and perhaps your journey.

Realize that the journey doesn't stop at the end of the book but that it continues through the connections we make with ourselves and with the people we care about the most.

– Steve Fowler, February 2024

Chapter 1

CHAMELEON

The color of my skin is my biggest fear. It is not just about blending in visually, it is also about blending in tonally, verbally, and conceptually. It is a facade, an exhausting facade of always blending in.

I have been a chameleon for much of my life and career.

A chameleon, in this respect, is someone who is present but is intentionally unseen.

Someone who is skeptical of their surroundings.

Someone who fears their surroundings.

Someone who is waiting to see the dominant color in the room, and match that color as closely as possible.

I was eleven years old when I moved from India to the Chicago area in the mid-1970s when Chicago was just at the tail end of segregation.

My previous understanding of the United States was what I had seen in Western children's books: green lawns, Radio Flyer wagons, and blonde-haired kids with blue eyes.

My parents married and, as declared missionaries for the church, moved to Kathmandu, Nepal where I was born. My mom is a nurse and my dad is a medical technologist. Shortly after I turned a year old, we moved back to India where my parents continued their mission in the southern part of the country.

I have memories of climbing trees at that age as well as annoying my sister. I have very vivid memories of disliking having to hold my sister's hand and being dragged around.

In India, I started first grade at a Catholic school. I remembered the overwhelming presence of mean nuns. You had to get in line, say your prayer, get sprinkled with holy water, and then sit down for a beating with a ruler's edge. Sitting in the corner with a dunce cap was a real thing. We would get whacked with a paddle at least once a week by one of the nuns, and I hated that.

When I was around five or six, my parents had an opportunity to move and take on a mission in Afghanistan. This was before the Russians invaded and when Afghanistan was a monarchy under its own rule. I recall embracing Afghan culture as a child.

I recall our family, friends, and neighbors from the United Kingdom and the United States who also served the church mission. It was a blended community and I never noticed or thought about different skin colors. You might say I was blind to it.

Away from the rule of nuns, it was a different educational experience and story in Afghanistan. We were homeschooled by a Seventh-day Adventist woman from the United Kingdom. She was very sweet and gentle, she taught my sister and me along with her daughter and son, who were older than us. At that time, we began to speak Pashto (Indo-Iranian language) and Farsi as our secondary languages.

When we were living in Afghanistan, the low cost of services allowed us to have servants who lived inside the compound. They guarded our main gate, served as interpreters, and would do chores around the house. For a time, and specifically in that region, we were considered well-to-do; elsewhere, we were far from wealthy.

I remember befriending two little local boys who lived there and were close in age to me. We became friends very quickly, as I recall being fascinated by the language and the culture.

We would build toys out of things we found, like a toy truck with its axle and chassis made out of sticks that we tied together. We would use bottle caps for wheels and drag them around. We had fun and played all day together.

We lived ten yards from a main thoroughfare that was halfway paved, close to the hospital where my parents worked.

They were not concerned about us playing in or near the streets because that is what everybody did. All the kids were out there having a grand old time and my parents never worried about us.

Then we moved back to India in 1972 to a town called Ranchi, just outside Kolkata. We lived inside a compound which was specifically a Seventh-day Adventist medical community made up of medical professionals, theologians, and their respective families.

We never had to leave the walls of the compound, as everything we needed was there, including the church and hospital. The homes were tiny and made of stone, with dirt pathways, gravel, sand, and clay between the houses. There were some grass patches where we played field hockey, cricket, and football (soccer).

I was a lousy student and didn't pay much attention. All I wanted to do was play marbles, a very popular game at the time.

My parents would immediately know if I hadn't gone to school, I would have dirt all over my front pockets from playing marbles.

We had to wear a school uniform consisting of a light blue shirt and dark navy shorts, which I would wear with flip-flops or go barefoot.

I was always puzzled by how they knew I skipped school, but it's clear how they figured it out: from the dirt on my blue shirt.

My awareness of different cultures began at about eight or nine years old when I was told not to listen to the radio anymore.

In hindsight, with all due respect, how many traditional classical Indian songs with sitar can you listen to before you just kill yourself?

It is almost as annoying (to me) as listening to bagpipes.

No offense to anyone who loves that music, but to me, it is like a mosquito that will not go away.

At that age, I took my dad's crappy little shortwave radio that barely worked since it would receive the BBC.

At times, I would go out past my home and into the thick brush of bamboo bushes to hide and listen to the BBC Music Hour on the radio.

The quality of the audio was terrible, but it was the best thing I had ever heard in my life.

I was introduced to the Beatles by my best friend Anand while growing up.

He was a natural comedian and he and I would laugh and play together. Both sets of our parents loved that we were friends, but they also hated it because we would get into so much trouble.

I soon loved the Beatles just as Anand did, especially the song 'Let It Be', and I could not get enough of their music.

My community and family considered the Beatles the Devil's music and the guitar the Devil's instrument.

When my dad would catch me listening to this music, there was hell to be paid.

He once caught me listening to the Beatles' song 'Lucy in the Sky with Diamonds,' and he freaked out because he knew it was an acronym for LSD. This only embellished his idea of how it was devilish and sinful music.

You could say that the Beatles started the rebellion within me. When my dad and I would go shopping, he would not even let me look at guitars.

But when he wasn't there, I would see a music store and be fascinated, I would pretend that I was one of the Beatles.

Since I could not have a guitar, I made one.

We used to fuel our cooking stove with kerosene which came in these little tin, rectangular cans. My parents would toss them after they were done, so I got creative.

To create my guitar, I whittled the top of a stick to create a 'fretboard,' jabbed it into the top end of the can, put little tuning pegs at the top of it, and then used rubber bands.

This guitar stayed hidden in the bamboo field.

When I would go out there with my radio, I would jam out with this little guitar.

This made me feel like I could do whatever I wanted despite what my dad said.

I was free to do it in my arena, with a crowd of bamboo as my audience.

This was my shelter.

I continued to build other guitars out of whatever I could find. I even found some strings that were thrown away, which I would then take and try to use on my clumsy little guitar.

My parents did appreciate music of the 'right' sort and tried to get me to play the piano. I hated the piano, I only wanted to play the guitar.

Looking back, I regret not taking piano lessons. I think I could have been a much better guitar player later in life if I had, but I didn't have the desire to conform to what they wanted me to do.

This also marked the beginning of when questions about my family's and community's religion started to creep into my head.

Every time I was challenged, either by physical abuse, verbal abuse, or cultural, corporate, and social restraints, I would find some way of building a little kerosene-can guitar; to say 'fuck you' to the establishment and to jam out in the bamboo to 'Lucy in the Sky with Diamonds.'

When I was eleven, we moved to Chicago where survival was key.

We arrived there in the middle of summer, so I had a couple of months to acclimate. We didn't have neighbors who would interact with us, although many of my classmates lived in my neighborhood.

I was excited about the first day of school. It was a new place with new surroundings. I also hoped a red Radio Flyer would be waiting for me.

I was ready for everything I had seen in the children's books about growing up in the United States.

I was excited, I didn't see myself as different. Even at eleven, I did not distinguish skin color.

I learned quickly that I was different, that was the start of three years of bullying at school.

I won't dwell on this too long, but looking back as an adult, I am shocked at how little care or support I received from my parents, the church, and society.

After being beaten up by some of the boys in the youth group, my church's pastor said to me, "Yeah, I see that you are pretty bruised up, but this must be God's will."

Holy fuck.

That is when I blew up inside.

I remember that being a clear demarcation of time for me.

I doubted myself. I don't know if there were any clinical ways of determining whether I was depressed or not back then, but I definitely doubted my self-worth.

I was in a very dark place, I was questioning the value of myself, and whether or not to remain alive.

I decided that I needed to see for myself whether there was any truth in God's will.

I wanted to know if heaven was separated between a ghetto side and a picket fence side.

I wondered if the picket fence side would be all white people if there would be such a thing.

Maybe, as the pastor told me, there was 'the mark of Cain' that everybody seemed to inherently understand; all dark-skinned people were the murderers of Abel.

Maybe I would be considered good enough to make it to heaven, but not on the picket fence side.

This was such a pivotal and internally contested time for me since I had been so enamored with the faith that I wanted to be a pastor.

I thought I would be a good pastor since I loved playing the guitar (which I had finally been allowed to pursue).

I would lead youth activities in the church, where there would be singalongs and I would play the guitar.

I would also tell stories from the Bible, and I would have an audience.

I thought, 'Wow, I have their attention. These people, these kids, are actually listening to me and they are paying attention.'

I thought I had a skill in entertaining and that I would be able to pursue it over the years.

But was it God's will that I was to be bullied?

The Sabbath is the Holy Day and you do not bully people on the Sabbath, you have to be good.

Ironically, the same kids who would listen to me play music at church were the same ones who would bully me during the week.

I soon realized that the pastor of the church was using me to lead the songs because they didn't have a youthful leader who was passionate about the Bible.

He would say, "Yeah, do the singalongs, do the storytelling."

He was also the same pastor who had told me earlier that my experiences with bullying were because of God's will.

This catapulted me into a state of questioning everything.

As it turns out, that was a true gift.

I decided to read the Bible for myself. The first time I read it was how a religious person would have you read it, with sacredness and love for God and the Bible, where every-thing written is the truth and nothing should be denied.

The second time I read it, I tried to read it more critically.

The third time I read it, I was 17 and intentionally wrote some notes on the contradictions I had found.

I never shared them with anyone.

I wanted to fit in with the church, but I also wanted to challenge it and do it in my own way.

I was learning to be a chameleon.

I was bullied for three years, from when I was 11 to almost 14. At that point, I was just trying to discover my place in the world.

Imagine you are a 14-year-old, looking around and think-ing, 'Man, I just want to ride my bike. I just want to tool around with other boys, throw our bikes down, go into 7-11, grab a Slurpee, and talk about useless stuff.'

I didn't have that, but I would see other boys doing it.

I was afraid of approaching them.

There was a Dunkin' Donuts, which was very popular when we were kids, not far from where we lived. You could get a dozen donuts for only two dollars then just ride somewhere and hang out with a bunch of other friends.

I had my own bike, but I never fit in. My bike was old, not shiny or flashy.

It seemed people always knew that I was riding that bike because I would notice the other kids riding away from me.

I remember sitting down on our lawn with my bike lying flat and thinking, 'What is it going to take for me to join in?'

There was a deep need to be social, which I think is normal for a child. I had not been an introvert growing up, but I became one as a result of these years in my life.

I do not remember if I cried about it or not, but I knew I was deeply saddened and I did not sleep. I would wake up and think, whatever it took, I just needed to be like the others.

This was the seed of my loss of identity.

I did not know who I was, but I needed to make myself like them.

'Them' was nebulous, 'them' was everyone, and 'them' was never singular.

It was the community and it was wherever I resided.

It was wherever I looked or moved.

It was blending in for survival.

My own identity was starting to form, and this identity was more about not knowing who I was.

I transitioned into being okay with not knowing who I was. This was when I realized that people were only paying attention to me when I fit into what they expected me to be.

It became a reward system for me. When I would get a returned smile, that smile validated the fact that I was okay.

This grew into a facade I called my chameleon skin, or behavior; where I realized that the more I became like one of them, the more I was seen as successful, accepted, and welcomed.

'Welcome' was not so much as welcoming me into their homes. It was enough for me to be able to stand on the front porch and have a conversation and to be able to throw a football or play catch together on the front lawn.

Enough for them to say, "Hey, yeah, we'd like to pay you to mow our lawn." Enough for me to say, "Hey, Mrs. Jones, how are you today?" without being afraid. I dropped the Indian accent very quickly.

I would no longer eat the Indian food my mom prepared for me, instead, I made my own sandwiches. A grilled cheese sandwich became my go-to because I did not want to smell like an Indian. I did not want to sound like an Indian. I did not want to look like an Indian. I didn't have the concept of a chameleon back then, but I knew that I had to do that in order to feel validated and survive or even be considered successful.

My identity needed to be whatever people needed it to be, I realized, and I was intentional about it.

Since I was concentrating more on my survival and fitting in than my scholastic future during that time, my grades suffered. My future was more about the immediate.

I was only concerned about my ability to survive to the following day rather than looking out for my future success. At that point in my life, I realized that my smile had a kind of power, and that power just invited me to keep using it. This is not me bragging at all.

I just started to see that it was something I would be able to use as part of my toolkit. If people saw me as different, maybe I could use this to blend in.

I hate to use this word, but it felt like I was charming 'them' in some way. This charm was working, a facade that I needed to sustain.

This facade was to smile more, even with fake smiles. Whatever charm I had, I leveraged, to get what I needed and to avoid pain.

Even when somebody would say negative things about me, I would respond to the negative things with self-deprecation, using humor and laughing it off.

I found that humor would soften the issues surrounding race or acceptance. It made their words less harsh for me and, I think, even less harsh for them. This was a transition point in every conversation.

Fast-forward to 2015. I had one of the greatest managers in the world. His name is Steve deRham, a precious soul. He was a very confident and attractive man, about three or four years older than me, and his best friend was Indian. It felt like he understood me.

He asked me one day, "Steve, why are you so hard on yourself? Why are you so self-deprecating? When you get up on stage, why do you knock yourself down?"

I am paraphrasing heavily, but he told me, "Nobody likes that. It doesn't sound right. It may get a few chuckles here and there, but I guarantee that those chuckles are people that cannot empathize with that deprecation or racial biases."

This made me think back to why I was doing it.

When I was fourteen or fifteen, I wanted what every boy wanted which was a wrench in one hand and a jalopy stock car to work on.

There were shitty cars all over the place, people working on them just to get them to move another mile. We lived in an affluent neighborhood just west of Chicago, but it was not like today where teenagers have many different experiences on the whole.

You would get your grandpa's old car. I wanted to be like the other boys and learn how to repair my own car.

I specifically asked my dad and begged him to give me his old car. By the time he gave me his car, I had gotten my wish. It was broken and did not work at all.

Then I started working with other kids and seeking their mechanical knowledge.

Even at that age, you respect adults. But, I respected adults differently; I feared them.

Not like the fear of God, I had the fear of 'Holy shit, are they going to kick my ass or approve of their kids kicking my ass?' I would rather approach a kid and just fear them, rather than fear their parents.

But I was determined to be able to fit in, and it started with learning about a monkey wrench.

That monkey wrench turned to other tools, and those tools became conversations.

Those tools became an understanding of each other, and what limits there were in being accepted by them.

It became an understanding that it was not their own beliefs but their parents teaching them to isolate themselves from us.

I started trying to figure out a strategy to deal with the parents.

I was about 17, and at that moment, I realized that I had to be strategic and grow my mind.

And I had to smile.

My parents were very willing to pay for my sister's college education, and while I do not know how they managed it, they put her through private school to become an MD.

Today, she is a successful oncologist. They are extremely proud of her.

Everything they say and imply exudes their pride because she followed their instructions and the path they laid out.

I did not follow their path. I got some help for college, but most of it was paid for on my own. Instead, I decided to go into electronics and took a vocational electronics course. I had an Atari 800 that I was writing games for. I was fascinated and excited by the simple code that would light up the screen the way I wanted it to.

I bought a PC that was compatible back then, and it had a bootlegged copy of the MS-DOS operating system.

I was enamored by this little tiny computer that allowed me the power to access the hardware and be able to manipulate it.

I moved to the West Coast, living with my cousin. I went on to Oregon State University where I got a computer science degree since I was determined to work at Microsoft.

I thought there was no way in hell I was going to get a job at Microsoft because I put them on a pedestal. I just never thought I would have access to an opportunity like that, but then I got my first internship at Microsoft.

I went back and finished my computer science degree in two and a half years and then joined Microsoft in a new product division.

It was exciting to transition into the corporate scene, and I was all about being in the moment.

The Internet was not as pronounced as it is today, where we take it for granted.

Today it is seen as a necessary utility. Back then, only privileged people, universities, and the government had access to the Internet.

Somehow, I realized that the trend was moving towards software. I knew that the power of this PC was empowering people like me.

I thought I could not be the only guy thinking this, so I jumped on the bandwagon and placed all my bets on it. It was analysis, strategy, self-preservation, and self-driven moments that got me to where I wanted to be.

My role at Microsoft was a very small role and my first true corporate experience. Microsoft had maybe only

2,500 employees at the time, you could walk around the campus and recognize everybody during the day.

I befriended a guy who sat next to me once and who befriended me very openly. I never felt that he had any hatred or disgust for me or even biases, so I felt safe with him.

We became best friends, doing pretty much everything together. We are still friends today, getting together every so often.

His friendship was great because it allowed me to study his 'wrenches' (his tools). This is how I survived.

I would do some intelligence gathering before I would go into meetings, even though I was not brought into bigger meetings or more exclusive meetings with corporate.

During the internship, I was supporting a product called 'Microsoft Word' for DOS.

There was no UI for it yet, and it was painful to look at. It is comical to think about that today, given how ubiquitous Word has become.

A name like 'Steve Fowler' helped me become a sort of natural chameleon.

Even today, when I need somebody to come over to fix something at the house, they are shocked when they see me, and appear to say, "Oh, wait, you don't look like a Steve Fowler."

They all have this bias.

The 'Steve Fowler' thing is a mask I can wear.

This even freaks out some Indians who say that I am not actually Indian.

I am stuck in this no man's land that allows me to be stealthy. It has allowed me to be able to pick up the phone without an accent, which I worked so hard to get rid of and say, "This is Steve Fowler. I need to understand how you do something. I need to understand your goals for this."

When I needed to make a phone call to support Word for DOS, somebody on the other end would think of me as 'one of them' because I did not have an accent to separate us.

The guy who sat behind me in product support was Malaysian. He also had an Indian background and a thick Indian accent.

You could tell that the customers would get irate by the fact that they were having to talk to someone who did not speak the way they did.

For me, I was reveling in the fact that I could masquerade as an accentless 'Steve Fowler' and not have anybody recognize whether I am of a different nationality or a different race.

This just emboldened me even more. Being a chameleon would help me intentionally blend in to understand what was necessary to succeed.

I would see somebody getting praised at work and I would want to get that praise as well.

I would circle popular and successful people, not getting to know them in person, but to see how and why they were successful.

Not only would I pay attention to the things they used, like tools on their PCs, but also what they read and what their eating and exercise habits were.

I would lurk in silence and pay attention to everything. This was not me intentionally being creepy, wearing my chameleon skin. This was just me naturally, curious about why he was getting all the praise, wondering why it was not me, and why I was not as successful as him.

I came across the notion that it's seen as success for others if you cast these perceptions. This drew me towards opportunity, something to take advantage of, a rinse-and-repeat situation.

I was successful at Microsoft, reaching the level where I was deemed a 'partner'.

You prove yourself as a partner because you have to be mentored and sponsored by an executive. They essentially start to groom you for larger things. This was a pinnacle of success because only a very small percentage of people made it to that level.

Money was not the driver for me, but I did make good money. I probably made the same as everybody at those levels, but my success felt more personal.

I did not flaunt my wealth, but I did splurge on things I could not have as a kid such as guitars.

I just went nuts and bought 13 of them, because I wanted to show my parents and be like, 'Fuck you. I can own a guitar now, and I can play it whenever I want to.'

Growing up and into my career, I compared myself to others who seemed to just naturally exist in this world without having to be a chameleon and have their desires met without adversity.

But I do think most people adopt chameleon-like behavior. While we can all relate to my story, perhaps it is with just a slight degree of variation.

We have all experienced racism, I am sure. We have all experienced denigration, I am sure. We have all faced our parents at some point. We have all been told not to do something we wanted to, and we found a way to do it.

This is really about what a waste of time being a chameleon is and, instead, just pursuing what you want.

Bill and Steve

I idolized the influential power that Bill Gates and Steve Jobs had. I wanted that, and I still do.

I still feel like I am not able to influence as well as I want to. It is a personal limitation, but I idolized their ability to influence the market and their ability to influence the people who worked for them.

The chameleon side of me thought, 'Well, I have got to start somewhere. I have to look back at where they started.'

I looked deeper and saw that they were assholes at the beginning. I did not necessarily see it as 'asshole' behavior, but as being so determined that they would not let anyone get in their way.

That is when I tried to mirror their behavior.

I felt the need to be an asshole because that is how it seemed like they wanted you to be in order to appear successful, especially at Microsoft.

Do you want something? Well, you have to push for it.

How do you push for it? You demand it. If they don't do it, then you can be an asshole.

Leaning into the asshole was reflected well in my end-of-year review. It seemed to resonate with them, and it seemed to get the results they wanted.

There is a great children's book called, 'If You Give a Mouse a Cookie'. If you give a mouse a cookie, he is going to want another.

If you give a mouse another cookie, he is probably going to want a glass of milk.

I was the same.

I was emboldened by the rewards of being a chameleon, camouflaging my true identity because that is what they wanted.

When I was trying to become like Bill and Steve, I would break down their success.

I would read their press releases and their financial statements. Even when I was working at Microsoft, you did not get to see Bill's actual persona.

There was no online CNN or CNBC back then; no place to go to find details about someone's successes or failures.

However, the financial successes and failures were all published in publications monitored or used by Wall Street.

Wall Street became important for me because I wanted the wealth, I wanted the riches, and I wanted the abundance that they had.

Bill bought his first Porsche, I had never known he was a car enthusiast.

I was enamored by that, so I researched Porsche. I thought, 'Fuck me. How do I buy one of these?'

Back then, this was equivalent to around a $500,000 car.

I thought, 'Man, this is fist over fist money. He is making this out of us.

Our overhead, in terms of cost to the company, was minuscule compared to the money he was making from software sales and subscriptions.' I had the experience of sitting with Bill in a meeting where he just showed up.

I remember him saying something like, "Email is just a fad. It is a consumer platform. The corporate world is never going to use email." We were working on an email product at the time, so what he said to us was very disparaging.

I started to emulate that part of his presence. He came in very bold and assertive as if he knew what the world's direction was going to be.

At that moment I would sit at my desk, work on something, and think to myself, 'What would Bill do?'

The Game

I started morphing into someone that others needed me to be so that they could achieve their objectives and goals.

There is an underlying need to mirror somebody in order to be accepted. I would tie myself to their coattails, and I would mirror them.

If they were seen as successful, I would follow them. At Microsoft, if I saw someone I admired, I would gravitate to them and look for ways to either work for them or work with them.

Thankfully, I was given some autonomy to do that, but much of that autonomy was self-created, done after hours or days.

I would have a beer with them or find a way of getting into their mind so that I could figure out how to be useful to them.

I just wanted some dangling part of them to attach myself to, almost like a parasite, sucking the same blood they were.

I figured out early on that if you mirror someone, it actually helps people connect better. Morphing into someone to help them achieve their objectives and goals is almost enslaving.

I know this sounds harsh, but I was enslaved to their success.

My own purpose was lost as my purpose became their purpose. I was morphing into someone else to help them get ahead.

I wanted to mirror their success and have them see me as successful.

If I found someone successful, I would latch myself onto them and help them continue to be successful. I was hoping that by being a part of the stardust they would leave behind, I would become a star myself.

But I realized at some point that there was a limit to my chameleon persona and that there was a limit to my risk-taking. I realized I needed to find my own identity because it was not working.

The Measuring Stick

Stature, status, corporate status, and title encompass all the measures of responsibility in the corporate world. Even when I was older in the company, I still felt young and didn't know what the hell I was doing or how to really and truly measure success.

My measure of success was the ancillary bits that could be publicly and openly measured.

There was also the personal measure, which was proving, 'Aha, parents, I am successful. I have a house. I have a family. I did not have to go to medical school to have what I have.' It was about fitting into the community.

Personally, I would also measure my success; ironically, not based on the 13 guitars or going from a C-Class to an S-Class.

(I do not have a Mercedes, by the way, I am a simple guy. Even with the abundance, I drive a Subaru. I just need a car to get from point A to point B, and it does not matter to me what I drive. I used to have luxury cars, but I have gotten rid of them just because I have daughters, and I want to set a precedent for them.)

My measure of success was based on what it takes to be perceived as successful and respected. It was masqueraded behind a veil of a personality that was someone else's and not my own.

Being a chameleon necessitated conforming to those measuring sticks in order to fit into the environment I was a part of.

The measuring stick made me view the world in terms of objectives.

I sought success for myself based on these measures.

Shedding the Skin

I was using self-deprecation at every opportunity in order to insert some humor into conversations.

I wanted to feel like I had common, perhaps even lesser, ground with others.

If someone called me a slave, I would agree with them. That is what they expect, and I would say it in a joking manner so it would take the razor's edge off those words.

I did it solely for the purpose of being invited into certain conversational circles because that was important to me. Who am I? What am I? What are my core values?

I started to revisit myself, my values, and my needs. I began to realize that one of the fundamental things that made me happy was learning from intellectual people.

They would share their perspectives in an intelligent and open-minded way with thoughts, questions, and answers. They sought out my opinion and it was eye-opening.

There is a fascinating transition when someone asks you about their values and they want to be validated; when you reflect on your own, you realize that we are all humans in this world together.

The shedding of my chameleon skin came from examining the root of where my values came from.

I dismissed all values that were based on religious biases or beliefs.

I removed, or at least put a line through, values that were given to me by my parents. I became more aware of what drove me, what made me happy, and what caused the charm behind the smile I carried with me.

The charm behind my smile was about my childhood self. I was reverting to being a kid again, to being curious. Curiosity became the leading indicator to leaving the chameleon skin.

I asked myself why I was doing this. I started to become more self-aware.

I realized that my own guise was creating self-deprecation in a broader sense, and that limited my ability to stretch my own curiosities because I was following or chasing somebody else.

This only started happening later in my life, when I was 45 years old.

So, what are you supposed to do with this, dear reader?

I recommend you reflect on your values and stay true to them. Take a sheet of paper and write down everything that you value. Everything.

It does not matter if it makes sense or not, just write it down.

In a second column, rewrite those things that you value that you think are deserving of your immediate attention.

In the third column, look at the things in the first column and prioritize them, keeping in mind the attenuation the middle column can provide.

This kind of exercise starts to open the door within your own mind. You start to see how you self-direct and how to become who you are.

Your subconscious speaks to you through these values that you did not realize you had until you wrote them down.

Once you start there, boom, curiosity kicks in. Boom, your happiness starts to surface.

Boom, your connections with other people become more authentic.

Find Your Niche

I came to an understanding, a defying, and a disgust of Bill Gates, even with all that he virtually taught me. Much of my life was misguided because of my fantasy of wanting to follow his path.

I enjoyed the learnings from Microsoft, it shaped my technical ability and thus, my career. But now I regret those years.

There is a podcast called 'Bill Gates and Rashida Jones Ask Big Questions'. In episode 5 of the podcast, Bill admits that he faltered in his early years, in not understanding the value of creativity, the human story, and poetry. Bill reflects on the failures of his past, admitting that he did not realize the impact of software on humans and vice versa until much later.

I think that was a realization for me; there is a purpose here beyond software, perhaps to help people. This is why I want to help mentor people on their journey.

I don't want them to waste as much time as I did.

Finding my own niche came through an exploration of a single word; compassion.

It was an awakening word.

In my daily work as a tech executive, we would have

customers who are sometimes on the other side of the virtual firewall.

You try to understand those customers' sentiments. Working at Al Jazeera, I had to learn what customers really cared about.

I realized that they were not going to have the same tools to express their sentiments to me and I had to try to understand them by placing myself in their shoes.

It clicked for me. Not only did it change the way I interacted with customers, but how I mentored my own employees. I found my niche. My niche is that I am a compassionate and conscious business leader, but I did not always used to be. The consciousness came from leading with customer compassion and driving my natural talent as an engineer.

I push the 'why' questions into the realm of compassion so that I can translate that compassion into data, and then into engineering tasks and objectives.

Finding your niche softens you and creates a more humanistic you. You engage more with the people around you, professionally and socially.

You become more active in listening, more active in participating, and more active in finding each other's needs. Those are powerful things. Once you understand, once you can empathize and show compassion, people open up and share their vulnerabilities much more effectively and efficiently than ever before.

If you act like an asshole, you come up to someone and say, "What the fuck? What is wrong with you? Tell me what your day is like. I don't give a shit if you're having a bad day or not, but just tell me what your day is like?"

There is no compassion there.

You could take a different approach and say, "Hey, how are you? How's your day? I see that you're limping a bit, are you okay?"

It takes a different role than the asshole approach. You have to find the meeting point between confidence, empathy, and compassion.

When you do, there is a sharing of vulnerability. Small as it may be, this is a gain that you personally achieve. This is intelligence that you can gather to leverage your own success. Not even in a capitalistic way, although that is often the case in business, but in a personal way where you are building capital with and investing in that person.

The power of being a chameleon is the ability to shape-shift to fit in. We all want to be accepted and be part of a group or a tribe.

We pick a tribe and recognize ourselves as part of that tribe. I work at Microsoft, and I have worked at Apple. People hear you work at these large companies and they respond to you differently.

It was all about money and status. Shifting your mindset from what can be gained from it is essential to move beyond material satisfaction, which does not last long.

You get 15 minutes of fame, and then what? There is no substance left. What if the tribe leaves you? Your identity is still tied to the tribe, but no one is paying attention to you anymore.

Then what?

You realize the limits of being a chameleon when you recognize how exhausted you are from attempting to be accepted. Finding that limit is important when you have had enough.

You think, 'I am straddling this line. I am chasing after something that I am never going to get or achieve.

It does not make me a failure, and it does not make me stronger or weaker. I just have to find a path that is truly me. It goes back to values and staying true to them.'

So, what is it that you want in life?

You, personally. Not in your career, but just you. What do you want? Ask yourself what it is that you want, over and over again, until you develop a set of core values. Stop being a chameleon and figure out your purpose. Stop being a chameleon and focus on your values. Stop being a chameleon and find your own power.

Stop being stealthy.

Be powerful.

Chapter 2

INTELLIGENCE

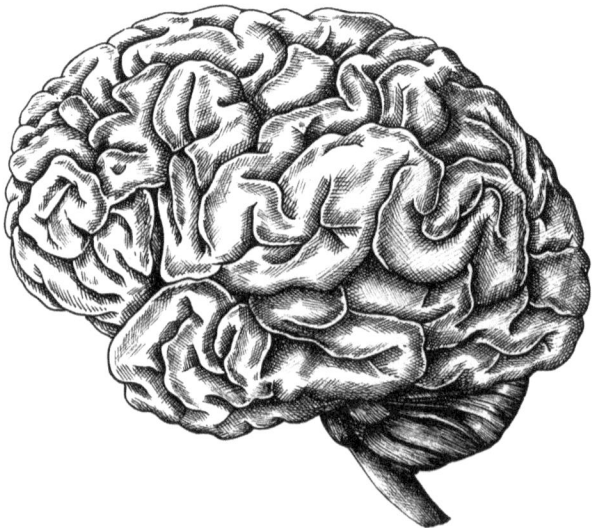

Gathering intelligence was about survival. But intelligence for me was also about sustainability and credibility. Arming myself with information was critical to how I navigated my goals, my successes, and my needs.

I wanted to capitalize on my success over anybody else's, which drove the 'asshole' behavior I wore like a cloak.

Understanding somebody else's objectives meant gathering more intelligence beyond the common shared objective, like having a product to ship or certain features we needed to enable.

I was also asking myself, 'What are their personal objectives? What is their agenda? Are they overthinking about their own fears and their own success, as I am? Who's going to win that mental argument?' It could be just a metaphysical presence, energy, or something else I needed to capitalize on.

I would strategize around that. If a person had an objective to learn more about my intelligence gathering, I would turn that around and ask myself, 'Is he intelligent?'

I would argue he is not as good at intelligence gathering as I am. I would break that down. It would start with a product or common objective and then go down further and deeper, towards a specific individual's objectives.

Knowing them would give me more clarity on what their objectives were. If I didn't know them, I would safeguard myself with a series of abstract questions and learn about them in quick sound bites to control the narrative.

The intelligence I was looking to gather was just a mental framework of things that informed me of my own security, of myself, or what I didn't know.

I was worried about the external perception of me, married to the goals and objectives of the next six months or a year. I was concerned about an attack on me personally, so I had to shield myself with a moat of intelligence.

I was intentional about only seldomly and strategically dropping the drawbridge for a specific person to let them into my castle.

I created my own container of information, based on what I gathered from observing other people. This container was filled with information on personalities, agendas, objectives, and urgency.

The urgency was twofold: the urgency of driving to some success, but also the urgency to protect my own fear.

My tactical method for intelligence gathering involved writing someone's name down, later looking them up in the address book, and I would see who they reported to and look at their status in the company, the size of their organizations, and the products that they were responsible for.

If I didn't know someone personally, I would hopefully find some mutual acquaintance with that person, like a third-degree connection or even six degrees of separation.

I knew that it was going to be anecdotal and that much of it was going to be hearsay. I would ask questions about that person, and look for common words in their responses.

I would ask questions about how long they had been at the company, or how long they had worked on a product.

I would ask questions about tenure because that meant they were valued at the company and had continual support for their growth.

I would also look for how quickly they'd grown within the company, which was a sign of their personal ambition. This helped me understand how aggressive or tenacious they were.

I put so much work into the feedback I would seek out, looking for common words and seeing if those words were translatable into personal values.

For example, if one person said, "This person is an asshole; I don't like him" and somebody else said, "He's a nice guy, but he's sort of a narcissist," I would pair those values together.

I would put stars or asterisks around these values, and I would write, 'Product X, experience X, asshole X.'

I would put a one to five rating for each.

Then I would go on to the next person, and the next person, and the next, doing the same.

If there was a senior employee who was above my pay grade, I would relax a little bit, thinking, 'Well, they have their own agenda. I've got to respect it and leave it alone.' It didn't mean that I couldn't gather intelligence, it formulated how and when I would reach out to these people and create deeper relationships if I needed to.

For me, those relationships were all professional and mostly superficial. If they were a bigger asshole than me, I wanted to keep my distance from them maintaining a superficial presence with them. The effects of this led to passive-aggressive behavior on both sides.

I was trying to apply street smarts to my intelligence gathering. I wanted to find ways of involving myself and shaping, maybe forcing, some influence on the meetings I was in.

I wanted to combat my apprehensions or fears through adversarial behavior. The more I behaved and sounded like a bully, the more attention I got. It was kind of like being a gangster, where you're trying to figure out where your enemies are and where you're going to benefit most.

If I'm selling drugs on the street, I want to know where my competition is.

I want to know what their weak points are. If I have to pull out my gun, I'm going to pull out my gun. That 'gun' was my asshole behavior.

It was exhausting.

Emotional intelligence gathering is just a bitch.

This was more important to me than understanding how well a product needed to be managed.

I was managing myself more in this intelligence gathering than I had realized. I thought I was doing more to affect direction because of my success criteria, but what I was really doing was protecting myself and acting on my fears more than anything else.

Gathering intelligence was a waste of time, it yielded very little at the end of the day. As I look back, I wasn't myself, I wasn't authentic, and I wasn't the person who was passionate about what I was doing.

I wasn't showcasing my own competencies and capabilities, standing out on my own, or recognizing that my diversity of thoughts could have aided the conversations in a different way.

I was focusing on the wrong problems because I was protecting myself, I wanted to blend in, and also because I needed external validation.

But it also helped me accelerate relationships much more effectively. It helped me hone my observational skills, and my ability to read people, and connect with them. It shaped my ability to turn on my charm and smile when the smile was effective and mirror that person to my advantage.

When you mirror somebody, like we all tend to do with the people in our lives, it creates a deeper connection. The intelligence gathering actually helped me accelerate more than I would've had if I had just come into the room empty-handed without any of that intelligence.

At the time, it felt rewarding when I came out ahead.

There was external validation when my manager, or whoever, would say, "We nailed that goal."

It was an accelerant for me.

The reward was having a deeper connection with someone.

One of the things I enjoyed most was when I found somebody that I got along with and knew that they were someone I would want to work with in the future. It gave me more confidence than I would have had otherwise.

Now, back to my approach to intelligence gathering, for better or worse.

Personalities

When I gathered information about a person that I didn't particularly know, I would associate the information with a value system.

Then, they would fit nicely in a little container I put them in, whether it was, 'This person's a blockhead', 'This person's round', or 'That person's made out of jello, they're just squishy and not really decisive.'

There were multiple containers such as the objective, the agenda, the urgency, and the personalities.

With each new meeting, there was a new container or sub-container.

Some of the sub-containers on individuals would persist only because I either admired them or hated them.

When I was gathering intelligence on people's personalities, I also had three categorizations for people: I knew them, I barely knew them, or I didn't know them at all.

If I knew them, I wouldn't necessarily create a container for them. I would just think, 'This asshole is coming to the meeting', or, 'It's great that this guy's coming to the meeting.'

If I liked them, I would reach out to them and ask, "What are your objectives from this meeting? Did you see this agenda?"

I could then formulate my strategy, whether it be partnering with them or coming in to challenge some of their thinking.

It was necessary for me because challenging their thinking was my way of trying to assert more information about our agenda.

I could have easily done this in an email, saying, "Hey, I'm going to challenge you on some things."

Yet the asshole part of me wanted to show them in front of others that I've actually thought through this much more.

I was really, really determined in that way and would do my homework.

I would make sure that I was not going to say something that was just ideological or that some platitude was unachievable. I would look for clarity.

At the time, I felt one of my strengths was storytelling. I wanted to tell the story of the customer and our product. If that story for the product didn't resonate with the workflow, I would question it and I would argue. I wouldn't hesitate to engage and manage expectations to some degree. For those that I had to interact with but didn't know well, I would look for purpose.

I would figure out what their purpose was, so I would go around them and go talk to people that they knew. If I didn't know anybody that knew them, I would put them in the category of 'I don't know this person'.

It took much more to figure out who this person was.

If I were to estimate, gathering intelligence from the people I didn't know would take 25-30% of my day. That amount of time spent, and the subsequent lack of time actually being productive, was exhausting and a failure.

I was trying to manage everything in an eight-hour day but was ending up working fourteen hours a day. As I got older, the transition from young Steve to the older Steve honed my observational skills. I could read patterns in people and make assumptions much more quickly.

Agendas

I always wanted to know what the objective of a meeting was. I wanted to know whether or not we were going to come out successful, and whether or not I was going to come out successful.

If you want to go for a hike, you think, 'All right, I'm going to go hiking, and this is the path we're going to take with no deviation', it's very simple.

You don't want to get lost in the forest and you want to come home safely.

You stay on track and on the path.

If there were items brought up in the meeting that weren't on that agenda, I wasn't prepared to talk about or engage in those things.

I found reasons to dismiss anything outside of the agenda.

I would go about gathering information on agendas. If an agenda item didn't make sense, then I would reach out to the person and ask, "What specifically are you looking for with this?"

I was a big subscriber to a process that was used at Microsoft called 'Precision Questioning and Answering.' It's about delving five layers deep as possible into everything. With that, I was always prepared to give the answers and if there was no prior precision there, I would ask or seek it out myself.

Gathering intelligence on agendas gave me a shield to protect myself. It was the initial step; it gave me the Batman suit. It gave me an understanding of who my favorites were, working and partnering with them, and even triangulating around them.

It protected me from the unknown environment by preparing me with the right tactics to manage the meeting. It made me feel more confident.

If I didn't have that Batman suit on, I would feel vulnerable and much less confident. I would literally visualize my tail between my legs and be whimpering internally if I didn't have that protection.

I spent more time than was necessary working to understand everyone around me.

I should have allowed people to either like me or not based on my own merit.

I should have had a stronghold on my own objectives. There's no denying that. It's something I still do today, seeking clarification on a shared commitment or shared objective.

I didn't allow anybody else to clarify; I wanted that clarity for myself, I was the driver.

That clarity drove my own internal agenda because I wanted to come across as successful. I wanted to come across as the leader.

It was exhausting because not allowing diverse thought or conversation put constant pressure on me, as opposed to allowing organic thought and leadership to occur.

Objectives

I needed a starting point for my intelligence gathering. It gave me what I needed to enter a conversation or a room. If there weren't any shared objectives, I would question whether my time was needed there or not.

Objectives were to be common, measured, and shared. Goals were often bestowed upon us, whether a particular product or a marketing objective. We broke them down into every activity.

For example, let's say the objective was to increase the performance of our product by 'X' number of users and 'X' number of seconds per transaction.

Interdisciplinary actions would come out, and I would sit in meetings where we would divvy out who's going to do what. A product manager would be in charge of certain things, like investigating a technology so that we would be able to leverage it. They would write the specifications and we would then negotiate those specifications based on our competency or accessibility of a particular technology. That drove the separation of responsibilities. We'd come back and check in with each other, making sure we were on target for the objectives asked of us.

This became another personal protection thing for me. It took more precedence to figure out the people.

I didn't understand, like project managers, marketing people, or anybody else who was foreign to my discipline.

I wanted to make sure that they viewed me as being the successful leader I was and that I was also putting myself in their shoes as well.

It was essential to know who they were and what they cared about to help me understand how I needed to pander to their situation or needs.

Cognitive ability was paramount to me. I would judge people on whether their arguments sounded logical, whether their problem-solving skills were acute, or whether they were accepting of learning new information and adjusting accordingly.

While somebody dreamed up an objective, my first reaction was, 'Is this meeting aligning to the product and the product cognition? Does it make sense? Or is this just another meeting?' I hated meetings because I had to do all of my intelligence gathering beforehand.

The rewarding side was a good or sincere 'thank you' from somebody, an email that said, 'I really enjoyed the questions', or the positive commentary. That was my incentive and reward.

But there were also many failures because I would over-think a situation.

I'd feel disparaged because I didn't feel validated.

Sometimes I didn't need to do as much intelligence gathering as I did. It was so exhausting as I spent such a large percentage of my day trying to figure out every character that was going to be on stage.

The fear of not knowing led me to overthink a situation much more than was needed.

I would even find myself overthinking my own assessment of someone. That was really exhausting, but I didn't realize it at the time.

Urgency

Looking back on how I gathered intelligence, it reminds me of merging your car on the highway. You have to match your speed to the other cars.

I wanted to understand the other person's speed.

If I knew that a highway was going to be filled with unnecessary traffic or roadblocks, I would find a different route, searching for the easy, frictionless road to go as fast as I could.

I saw all the other drivers as idiots because they didn't know how to drive as quickly as I could. Speed was a point of pride for me to showcase and urgency became an important consideration for me.

Every product has a milestone. There is a target date, and you have to consider what's possible and what's not possible.

You have to figure out what 'urgent' means in each case.

You have to pay attention to the people that fill the void of impossibility with bullshit, those who are trying to throw smoke and mirrors to avoid the scorn of not being able to meet deadlines.

The urgency was always to make sure that we were delivering on time. I was in charge of leading them to ensure it.

As I grew in my career, I had to manage the budget, which became another urgency. You don't want to waste money on missteps so there becomes accountability for urgency.

Gathering intelligence gave me a sense of confidence and protection despite my long work hours and the impossible urgency everywhere else.

That was empowering for me. It protected my instinctual fears at the time.

It was as if I was in traffic, using the metaphor from earlier, honking my horn or hitting the gas, feeling more powerful than the other drivers on the road.

My intelligence gathering helped me to manage, manipulate, or manifest what was needed in any situation, no matter how urgent it was.

It also resulted in me trying to take control of my own life. I was trying to achieve a certain mental state of feeling free of the external circumstances that were out of my control.

I was trying to manage these forces in a very finite way and cultivate some level of self-awareness, 'This is Steve's identity; leave me alone.' This was my castle, I was in charge of it. I already mentioned the moat surrounding it and the drawbridge that was up most of the time.

If you wanted to set up a time with me, then I was going to bring my castle along because I felt safer in it. But lugging around a castle in your backpack is pretty tiring.

This castle was filled with antiquated methods and a daunting set of implements for intelligence gathering.

I actually believe people would see me come into these meetings, guarded inside of my castle, which created limitations of having fluid, meaningful conversations.

I would most certainly expect other people to think that my intentions were contrived, pre-notified, and preset; and that there was no room for much of a debate unless that debate fell into my expectations.

When I think about defining the characteristics of power, it's when you control your own life and your own experiences.

As a result, you have increased satisfaction, confidence, and resilience. You become much more empowered to shape your destiny when there is self-awareness, cognition of the limitations, or chameleon-like behavior to adapt.

If I limit the chameleon and chase something or someone that is out of my control, I'm compromising my values. I'm compromising my own power. I'm restricting it.

I think it leads to a loss of authenticity, and I become enslaved to my own limits. I didn't embrace my own truth. Instead, was living as others expected. It was controlling my persona and my life. It affected my overall fulfillment of what I seemed to need. I wasn't really happy.

I think it's critical to prioritize and cultivate more self-control. Safeguarding your own well-being has to be transformative.

You have to understand your emotional well-being and then you have to work to break free of the external circumstances that you cannot control.

Self-control is paramount and it fosters positive well-being. A strong sense of self-control over your life is a reliable indicator that leads to overall happiness and contentment, especially when you let go of all external factors. It's about saying, "Yes, I need to let go of something. I need to let go of a bunch of shit I'm carrying in my head that doesn't make any sense."

We all have survival instincts.

As humans, we have an advantage that goes beyond a reptilian reaction to everything.

We can enter into a learned and open mindset that allows us to begin by learning about ourselves.

Learning about your limits and your own personal powers, and incrementally working through your limitations with the goal of seeking your own personal happiness has to originate within.

Someone else can't make you happy.

Someone else's validation is short-lived.

Personal validation and acknowledging your power are much more effective and longstanding.

Chapter 3

STRATEGY

As innocent as they may have been, I always thought that every white person was ready to shoot me for some reason. I never knew whether they would be able to accept me in their space or if they were going to say, "You have the mark of Cain. You're the guy who's never going to heaven. You're going to be forever doomed."

I didn't want to be doomed.

How do I combat my inner will not to be doomed and to win at least some degree of victory?

The goal was to get accepted, which is why I became a chameleon.

My own Trojan horse.

I wanted to blend in and pretend I was white, even though I wasn't.

I saw it as a form of validation when I would go to Texas for business and have meetings with this one particular guy.

He would always introduce me as "This is Steve Fowler, but he's one of the nice guys. He's okay."

What the fuck does that mean?

Later, I realized that he was introducing me to his white friends as a guy who is dark-skinned but acceptable, "He's okay. He is one of us."

I think it was innocent, but it was still ingrained in him as something he had to do. He had to defend his friends, who were not the kind he would usually hang out with. He invited me to go hunting at 4:00 in the morning. I'm not a person who typically goes hunting. Sometimes after a boar hunt in Texas, they put the pig on a fire, rotate it as it roasts, and then celebrate around this fire.

You start roasting around 7:30 in the morning and crack open your first beer. This is what you would expect with a Confederate flag waving behind you.

They're rotating the pig throughout the day, laughing it up and drinking cases of beer until 4:00 p.m. when they're ready to eat.

When I first arrived that morning, the crowd went quiet. I felt like I didn't belong there.

But my Texan friend stepped out of his chair, quickly moved towards me, and said, "This is Steve Fowler. He's one of the good guys."

I had to stage all my interactions and act within others' expectations. I always had to be on guard when engaging with every person.

As I mentioned earlier in the book, I feel like my smile has a certain charm and could be used as part of my stealth toolkit. When I smile, people tend to respond well. Their guard dropped a little.

When I knew that there was more tension than I knew what to do with, I would just keep smiling. I would even denigrate myself, telling jokes about myself and my skin color.

I would try to lower myself to their level of thinking so I would feel accepted and be seen as funny.

How degrading is that for me personally?

I felt less confident about who I was.

It was a show that I had to perform for every single person in the room.

♟ ♝ ♞ ♟

When I moved to the United States, I was reaching puberty and found myself only attracted to white people.

I guess it was me trying to project that I wanted to be white. There was a level of protection there and I wanted to fit in in every aspect.

I even ended up marrying a white person. She was blue-eyed, blonde, and fit in easily. I was thinking, 'What a perfect storm, right? I have a white person living with me; how cool is that, guys? Come on, give me some credit. I'm white, too.'

Don't get me wrong. I love my wife. She's a great mom, and I've got two beautiful daughters. They're amazing, and I get choked up just thinking about them.

The part of this that's really tragic is I had to engage at a level that almost dehumanized who I was for so long. I removed parts of my personality and mischaracterized myself for the sake of my own inner survival.

Nobody knew what I was actually like because it would morph. I was the chameleon. That was my strategy. I also had to morph once when I went into an all-Mexican neighborhood. People started speaking Spanish to me because they thought that I looked like someone from the Dominican Republic or one of the other islands.

I got validation from the fact that I could fit in wherever I needed to because I would mirror their behavior and they thought that I was 'one of them'.

It was just a weird space that I was not only in, but I was shaping.

My strategy was always to morph within a setting and that would then include multiple layers of attack.

I had my own fears and biases because of my experiences growing up, I would judge others based on the color of their skin as well.

It was unfair to them because they could have been great people; I didn't give them that chance because I was on the defense.

I was only on the offense if I saw any vulnerability in them. I would never share my vulnerabilities because that would show weakness.

That didn't equate to success for me.

My strategy started with survival.

I was constantly feeling like I was looked at and treated differently. In many cases, I was a first-hand witness to prejudice.

Just recently, a surge of my past self, the 'Old Steve', re-emerged. I was in Starbucks standing in line, loading my app, and trying to figure out whether I had points that I could use.

I looked up, turned around, and saw a guy with a big cowboy hat and a huge belt buckle that spanned across his hips.

He epitomized the kind of cowboy that would strike fear in me, and I thought, 'Oh man, this guy could be trouble for me.'

So, at that moment, the survival instinct kicked in, 'Shit, am I going to be treated differently?'

I looked at him a second time and he looked back at me with a cold stare. I felt myself stand up as tall as I could, broadening my shoulders and inflating my chest, trying to appear confident with my back facing him.

I then moved forward in the line, thinking, 'Nothing bad could happen in Starbucks.'

I started to question what my exit strategy would be if something were to happen. How would I turn around and run for the front door?

How would I react if he said something to me or stared at me again?

The rush of thoughts started a series of questions on how to survive first, and then how to overpower, or at least try to overpower, his perception of me.

I know these were unfounded assumptions. It was the 'Old Steve' coming through, coming up with the strategy I would build based on survivability.

What was ultimately fueling my behavior in that situation was the fear of not being accepted. I predominantly think that this strategy was my way of seeking validation for who I was.

I wanted to coexist, but with self-demands of success as a form of validation. My body starts to react viscerally and my emotions take over my thoughts. My thoughts become a series of questions: 'Do I come out of that meeting or interaction with a feeling of success?'

Success meant that I was respected and validated in my intelligence. If it wasn't working, then I would get boisterous, and try to fan out my feathers like a peacock would to put on a show.

At the beginning, the observation starts with the initiation, which is me smiling and gauging the charm of everyone.

If it wasn't working, I would keep a mental list of people who didn't respond well to my attempt at being charming and then would seek out different criteria for approaching each one.

Then there is the conquest. That's what a general would do. You start with what you need to conquer and then work backward.

The conquest consisted of what I needed to do to win or even knowing what victory looked like. It was a framework of how I viewed success, and what others, like my coworkers or boss, would deem successful.

I would start with that and then end with it. The conquering part of my strategy started with the criteria for success. Then, I would work backward to decide what needs to be done.

I would look for contextual observations and observe with particular attention to someone's ability to be in the room and whether they could provide predefined intentions.

If the agenda or the intention wasn't there, then I would need to know if I was going to waste my time with an individual or not. If they didn't live up to my expectations, I would dismiss them. I learned to recognize this through my own observations.

I observed everything from their knowledge of the space to their interest level, gauging their interest in this or that.

I would also assess whether they were an intern, a sophomore in this field, or if they were a senior; more so to observe the context of the meeting, or to even gauge my behavior or somebody else's.

Those were things that I needed to know, whether I should hold my shield up or if it was safe to keep it down.

I would always attempt some level of charm offensive to try and understand them. I would smile and see if I got a smile back.

I would then judge the smile to see if it was a friendly smile, an authentic smile, or a passive-aggressive sort of smile.

If the kind way or the charming way didn't work, I would scan the room. I would listen and observe for opportunities to attack, I would attempt to measure other people and think things like: 'Are they smart? Are they likable? Are their goals aligned with mine? Are they intelligent?

Are they exuding the behavior I need to get to my solution or end result?'

It was all about their ability to communicate. I paid no regard to my own ability to communicate. I would get frustrated when I wasn't getting what I needed from them in conversation, that's when I would interrupt them and be disruptive. If that didn't work, I'd be boisterous.

After launching the charm offensive, I would get a read of the room to see how they were accepting me.

If I noticed somebody in the room who was ignoring me, I would pay more attention to that person. They were now the center of my focus for validation since I didn't get it from them during the initial charm phase.

So I would pay extra attention to them and actually listen more to what they said, combatting it if I needed to or disrupting them more if not.

Perhaps I saw them as my competition, someone I should be afraid of, or someone that I shouldn't trust. I needed to decide very quickly on my approach with them. I would be disruptive, interrupting them if they weren't making sense, or they weren't aligned with my agenda or the context of the setting.

If that wasn't working, I would elevate my disruption by asking five questions. In my mental framework, I was aiming to get five layers deep when talking to someone, asking and asking them questions in order to figure out what they're really made of.

Then I would challenge them.

I saw challenging someone as different from being boisterous. I used a calmer tone to be disruptive, which meant that I would get away with challenging them more.

I would challenge their narrative. I would listen for precision in their questions or answers. If they weren't precise, I would look for ways to see if they were confident about their answer or their narrative.

If they weren't confident, it was a sign that I could either embarrass the hell out of them or dismiss them entirely. I would physically dismiss them by no longer looking at them and mentally check out from the conversation.

The Conquering

I always wanted to be ahead of the curve. There's a large emphasis on reviews and ratings at Microsoft.

They were extremely important, not only because of the emotional reward provided by your peers or your manager that comes with it but there was also a monetary reward, such as stock options or equity.

These were powerful incentives, but I wasn't as focused on the money aspect. Perhaps if I were, I wouldn't have been as neurotic as I became.

I was more interested in being ahead of that curve. On a scale of 1 to 5, the average person at Microsoft was 3.5. If you hit that 3.5, you were at the top of the curve, and people viewed you with the potential to either slide backward or forward. It was a much more nuanced slide forward if you wanted to grow.

The perception was everything.

If you created the perception that you were always ahead of the next person in terms of context, questions, leading answers, or whatever else to demonstrate that you were ahead of the average, then that was seen as conquering.

That was the modus operandi of conquering, and I would calculate what success would look like beyond the average performance. I would do a self-assessment of others who I gauged as being average and then I would go above and beyond them.

I needed the feeling of conquering the other people in the room. I needed to be better than them and I needed to visibly show that I was better than them. All of the other behaviors I have written about so far came from this need.

♙ ♗ ♞ ♙

When you bully your way through and see somebody crumble, it feels rewarding.

I felt gratification when I brought somebody down; I probably left a lot of people dead in my wake.

I drove a wedge in my relationships.

The wake that I created was all I reflected on.

I was thinking, 'How deep was it? How wide was it? How large were the ripples along the lake that I was motoring down?'

It felt rewarding and gratifying.

I gave constant attention to the reward or self-gratification, even when it was awful.

It was like a dopamine release to see how well I could lead this effort or these people towards me. It was about making sure that I left a conversation, meeting, get-together, or conference feeling like I led or even owned part of that narrative.

I had to pre-plan all the things that I had shaped in my head just to get to a point where I felt comfortable knowing that I was going to be accepted.

It was all about me being accepted, going back to my fears that everyone was rejecting the color of my skin. In turn, that further formulated my set of fears as someone who just wanted to be accepted.

When I was younger, I was just an innocent kid. I was always playing with marbles, wasting my time, and skipping school. I was the laziest student ever.

But I then realized that the way to fit in was to sort of push myself in there and to be a bully's bully. It was about that more than anything else. In my mind, it was about pushing, about bullying, in order to survive.

I was constantly finding that niche, that place of belonging for myself, the weakness in someone else, and the opportunity for me to accelerate my social standing.

I later realized that I could have done things slightly differently had I just accepted myself and gone into these situations knowing that I could succeed on my own merit, as opposed to trying to diminish or denigrate somebody else.

The Contextualization

I created a mental list of people's backgrounds, such as their educational history, as well as their merits in the company.

I did this in social settings, where I would look for measures that indicated their success, like social popularity.

This continued in the workplace where I would find measures like workplace influence, status, or stature in the company.

It was an artificial measure of someone before I engaged with them; I wanted to know the potential of their threat to me and how big this problem could pose.

In my self-assured persona, which was the insecure asshole Steve, I was responsible for my own demise. I created these structures that sized people, that judged them. I like to think we all are responsible for doing this, that we make judgments of people, thinking things like, 'That person's slimy', and creating a rating system to judge them in our heads.

At least I did. For example, I used to despise salespeople because all I thought they did was talk. I thought they talked because they were extroverts.

I always felt like I was more of an introvert, and yet, I couldn't let them talk more than me. I mean, that's just not Steve.

I had to assert some level of control so that I could come away feeling like I'd made my point with that person.

It was about predefining all these people, so I could go in and categorically address each one of them with the narrative I assumed they fit, the narrative I needed. If I knew someone was more shy or someone was more outgoing, I would adjust accordingly.

I would use shapes in my system to rate them, as a way to size them up. If someone was a square head to me, I would look at them or listen to them talk. I would think, 'God, that person's a geek', or 'That person's just a block-head'. Or I'd look at them as if they were a round ball and say, 'It's kind of cute, but I could slip around them. I don't need to spend a lot of time there.'

Or, I would imagine someone as a triangle or a pyramid and think, 'Wow, this person is multi-faceted. I need to spend time on each part of this facet because they're complex'.

Those I associated with the pyramid shape might have been someone that I admired because they had charm. They had a certain presence around them that I was attracted to, but I didn't know how to share or react to my attraction to them.

I prided myself on the awareness that I had to have around me. I was afraid of people. I was afraid of being accepted. I didn't even know how to be accepted, so I honed in on my observational skills.

Whether negative or positive, I honed in on someone's body language and how they responded to me. I tended to err on the side of negativity because of my insecurities during that time.

I still have insecurities, don't get me wrong. I'm not healed all of a sudden; I'm far from being healed. I developed this observation and this system of categorization only because I needed to figure out a way to position myself and survive.

It was always about survivability.

♙ ♕ ♘ ♙

When I was determining whether or not somebody is a pyramid, it was all about the initial charm they happened to exude. I don't know what it is, but I believe this is a universal experience: when somebody approaches you with a genuine smile, you just tend to melt internally and lower your defenses.

When somebody doesn't give you the time of the day, you pigeonhole them, you make these character judgments in seconds. In contrast, a genuine smile, even through my harshness and bullheadedness, just softens my heart.

When this softening occurred, I would feel, 'Oh, there is something about this person and I want to know more about them'.

My initial thoughts of being met with a genuine smile were always along the lines of, 'Wow, there's more to that smile', or 'That person is willing to engage with me. Is that person trying to pair up their facet with my facet?

Am I as charming as they are?'

These questions would immediately run through my head, and I would try to figure out how I could connect further with them, especially if it was someone who I felt was warm and accepting of me.

Due to my fears, I couldn't trust anyone. To be honest, I don't think I even trusted myself.

That initial smile slightly opened the door for me to think, 'Oh, maybe this person is genuine, maybe this person is authentic.' I would get to the point where I could interface with someone at the base level of their pyramid rather than just the top.

The difference between the base and the top is dependent on how broad of a personality a person has. If I don't see something beyond just the singular point on top of the pyramid, I'm going to dismiss that person for a while.

But if someone had a force about them, a really strong charm, I would seek to explore the base of their pyramid and notice each facet.

I would want to find out more and ask anything from "Hey, what do you do outside of work?" to "How did you get to where you are in your career? What kind of decisions do you make? How do you make those decisions?"

The things that I valued were around the ability to influence and I would be drawn to you if I thought of you as influential.

The Charm

I didn't know what charm really meant. I thought charm belonged to somebody else. I thought charm was something you were either born with or not.

I didn't realize charm could be developed. I didn't realize charm was something that could be honed. To me, the definition of charm is becoming more present with someone, spending time with them, getting to know them, and understanding them.

Everyone has a story. Everyone has their own needs. They all want to be successful and I want to share that success with them. I need to give a part of me to them to help them be successful.

When you're genuine in your actions and motives, I think most will accept the fact that you are someone who is present and genuinely cares.

There's an inherent warmth that comes with it too, almost 'Clinton-esque'.

Whether or not you like President Clinton, there's no denying he's a charming guy. He can convince the masses to jump off a cliff.

There's also a responsibility that goes along with leaning into the charm; you have to make sure you're leading the conversation in responsible ways.

It's all about being warm and present.

This is also where you can gain some of your own power. When you recognize that somebody is attracted to you, there is a power that goes with it, even a sense of empowerment. When you recognize that empowerment, you can do one of two things.

You can either take advantage of the person or you can help make that person feel like they are a part of you, part of the narrative, or part of the success that you are enabling.

♟ ♟ ♞ ♟

There is a big difference between charm and charisma. My smile has gotten me far. If I needed a person to soften, I would smile. I knew how to use my smile to soften the mood. That, to me, is a form of charm.

Charisma is more sustainable. It's the larger impression they walk away with, rather than just the first impression. It's more long-standing.

You might recognize the charm of the gray-haired dude

who smiled at you, but it's his charisma that makes you think, 'Wow, that guy was brilliant', or 'That guy was awesome to talk with, and I want to come back and talk with him some more.' I think I relied more on charm because my charisma was discovered much later and I'm still honing in on what it looks like for me personally.

Charisma is an important characteristic. I think it's more influential and my drive for influence was different from what I now think charisma allows.

Charisma allows influence in more peaceful ways than those that are aggressive or narcissistic, but I first learned that a smile at least got someone to open the door for me and let me in.

I learned the charm of my smile when I was getting bullied every day in school. I had to find a way to soften myself, show some level of vulnerability, to hopefully soften the next punch. If I looked hardened, if I looked angry, or if I looked troubled, I think it would have drawn more adverse behavior than what I was already receiving. But the charm also resulted in me changing who I was. I stopped eating curry, I stopped smelling like an Indian, and I started dressing like the people around me. I started to fit in like Romans do in Rome.

I just learned how to drop my accent, and even stopped speaking my native language to develop an American accent to fully fit in.

To me, I saw this as a necessity to the charm.

In business, the charm served me. By separating my fear from that charm for a moment, I realized that once I established a relationship with someone, my charm could take over in a less calculated way.

I would actually be less on guard with that person and so that charm was often an accelerator for me.

Still, I realized how exhausted I was at the end of every day. I used all the tools in the arsenal that I had, from a spectrum of charm to asshole and bullheadedness behavior. There were a variety of tools or ammo at my disposal that I would bring out. Sometimes, I would have to drop an atomic bomb and that was painful.

I would get rewarded for that sometimes, 'Wow, great bomb, Steve. That was perfect timing for dropping that bomb', or 'Man, you pelted that person really, really well.' My strategy of using charm was more akin to mirroring somebody. When somebody smiled at me, I'd smile back.

It was like the beginning of discovering people who fit my pyramid shape: people with enticing smiles.

I would want to get to know someone better, to see how the foundations of their pyramid were built, and then discover the various surrounding facets. It was the entry for using the charm.

So, back to my castle. I would drop my drawbridge for someone I saw as the pyramid shape immediately, inviting them in.

I wanted to get to know them more, to discover their intentions. That became part of my calculations for my strategy.

My strategy was related to those shapes that I described earlier. This is how neurotic I was; I would literally draw a shape on the notepad when I was talking to somebody.

I wouldn't write down their name, but I would draw a cube for someone I saw as a blockhead.

A person's shape had the potential to change.

There were times when I would recognize a square person was trying to let down their drawbridge for me from their castle. It led to a more charmed relationship or event because that person showed interest in me.

That person was no longer a square to me, but now a pyramid. I would then accelerate my relationship with that person because of it, honing in on them. They could become a person I'd want to lock arms with and go find ways to succeed.

If I understood how and where I could connect with someone, it was either an opportunity to denigrate or an opportunity to partner.

The Challenge

When I saw that Cowboy-type man in Starbucks that I mentioned earlier, I didn't feel comfortable around him. He reminded me of the oppression I faced as a kid.

I don't want to sound like a victim, but it just strikes a level of fear that I cannot fully describe. My brain immediately goes blank. It's like I'm entering a different part of the matrix, where it's only hollow.

The hollowness is me freezing. I don't know what happens to my body, but I completely freeze.

As soon as I come out of the initial freeze, I start to reach for the arsenal, for some tools to protect me. What should I do? Somehow I learned that if I stand up straight, I will look more confident. After taking that first step, I started to think about the type of language I would use to safeguard myself.

I'm only 5'8, so physically that person was much bigger than me. I had to prepare myself for a specific narrative or even look for an exit, as I had said.

I remember looking for ways to get out of line and just leaving the premises, thinking, 'I don't need my cup of coffee that badly. I'm leaving.'

It had to do with a degree of fear and what happens when that fear is invoked. In a corporate setting, I knew I was protected from the bylaws or policies within the company. I knew I had to be treated fairly and I would square myself with what 'fairly' means.

I know that I have had a reverse race projection because I fear all white people.

But why should I fear all white people? They're not all bad. Yet, I would just put them in a bracket.

When faced with a challenging situation, one which evoked a fear of mine, especially when it had to do with the way they looked or spoke, I immediately went to safeguard myself.

I realize now that we're all red-blooded people, all humans, who are trying to do what's right for ourselves. We're all just trying to survive in our own ways.

The main challenge was moving away from asking, 'Are they in a better place than me? What do they have over me right now?'

I didn't want that; I didn't want them to have control over me. It invoked fear and subsequently the narrative and my behavior.

♟ ♟ ♞ ♟

I was put in the partner program at Microsoft, which was a precursor to becoming an executive. It was treated almost as a public recognition in the company to be in this program.

The main focus was to help solve problems outside of just your own department. You would be paired with other Vice Presidents across the company, as well as having an executive sponsor.

My executive sponsor was Lisa Brummel, the senior VP of HR. She is very well known in the community there.

I soon realized that having this sphere of influence was changing me and I couldn't behave the same way as I did before when I could be more individualistic.

One of the VPs in the program asked me, "What are your values?"

I was asked to write it down and share it with them. Even though it wasn't the first time I'd been asked that question or even pondered it, it struck a chord for me that time.

What hit me was the realization that I needed to go back and evaluate my values often, not just once in my life, and call it good.

I had to constantly and consistently revisit my values. The values can be personal, professional, family, or spiritual. For me, taking that question seriously pushed me into a new phase of my life.

I spent the next couple of days reflecting on my values in a way I never had before. As I reflected, I got emotional and broke down. I recognized I had been chasing somebody else's values as opposed to my own my entire life.

Finally chasing my own, actual values led me to the realization, 'Okay, enough's enough.'

I left Microsoft within months of realizing that and it was one of the best things I ever did, I went to a company that didn't value assholes at all. They had a different culture than Bill Gates and Microsoft.

I eventually returned to Microsoft, coming back at the same level, but I felt that my values were important this time around. I maintained that my personal values were more important than corporate values.

Yet, I felt a pull to go back to my old self, so I left Microsoft again. This time, I went to Disney.

They're made up of artists and they think differently as a result. Most of the company, even the leaders, is media-centric with creative mindsets. They didn't understand an engineer like me coming in with more logical thinking.

It was a different, harsh awakening and a reality check for me. It caused me to reflect on my values again, and I decided on a new emergence of myself.

Those were the crucial moments in my career when I was reflecting on my values.

It's important for anyone who shares or reads this book to walk away knowing that they have their own values and should follow them. Be true to yourself, more so than somebody else.

The biggest limit is a self-imposed limit.

I was so focused on things I couldn't control, but I had the illusion of controlling them, and that's a limitation. Perfectionism is a neurotic behavior.

I was seeking perfection, which led me to another mental state, but not a good one, nor a healthy one. I tended to overthink.

Overthinking created additional limits because I was trying to control boundaries that were out of my reach. I was trying to grasp narratives I couldn't necessarily control. That was self-limiting because of my perfectionism and fear.

Fear is real, but also limiting, as my mind would spend more time rehashing the past and trying to rehearse some future than living in the present.

I didn't know what the future was, but I thought I did. I thought I was trying to create a future, but I wasn't. I wasn't present. I wasn't there. I wasn't listening. Those are all self-limiting factors.

The realization that all of this was a waste of time was empowering. I realized that I had to let go of all of this nonsense to find out that people truly and genuinely wanted to connect with me.

Those small beginnings became leverage, which became a power in a non-narcissistic or bullheaded way.

You have to understand your beliefs and you have to understand your values.

If you don't, you're going to enable your fears.

You build your belief system based on your fears and it's unfortunate.

Don't.

Evaluate your fears.

Chapter 4

BATMAN

In the Batman stories that feature Bruce Wayne as a child, he seemed normal. He had everything he needed and a supportive family. Then, when he lost his parents very suddenly, he was left on his own, left to his own thoughts and his own fears. He developed a huge fear of bats when he fell into the well.

My biggest fear wasn't bats, but it was going to school around the beginning of my teens. I was scared of getting out of the school bus to go to school.

Kids of my age in my classroom were like a colony of bats. I would panic at any movement too close to me, so I kept to myself because of what would happen after school or during lunch.

I had to very consciously keep myself in this protective bubble.

Because my bubble was always conscious and present, I struggled in school; I didn't pay attention to the teacher, I was paying attention to the fears.

As Batman grew older, he decided to pursue inner knowledge and self-identity. He went to Tibet to learn martial arts and uncover meaning in his life.

This paralleled my experience; I also didn't know what my own identity was. I didn't know what my place was, or what my role in life would be.

I was aiming for things that appeared empowering. I wanted to find something I could latch onto that would yield my own powers or help me find my own self.

My version of Tibet was my recognition of being Indian at the time and not wanting to be, trying to fight through it.

My Tibet was having a bully pretend to be my friend during church but share his disdain for me during the week and having to defend myself throughout the week.

There is a scene in the first Batman movie where the Tibetan house he was learning martial arts in burned down.

The burning down scene was significant for me when I watched that movie. I thought to myself, 'Wow, this is like me burning down my religious views.' It was burning down the bridges to my parents and my culture.

It was a fresh start for me. I'm going back home, but with a new vigor, a newly discovered me, and some-what of a rebirth.

I was 17 or 18 in 1982 when I decided to leave the church. The Batman trilogy came out much later, but the parallels were so significant for me that I sort of mimicked what I was seeing on screen.

I loved the safety of knowing that I could switch my personality to fit a situation as Batman did.

I didn't realize it wasn't healthy to do so, as Batman realizes later. I didn't realize that I had a couple of people in my corner, like Batman's butler, to really guide me.

By the third movie in the trilogy, Batman is beginning to be more comfortable with his own destiny by leveraging his past.

He recognizes it gave him some wisdom, perhaps not in the way that he should have pursued it, but nonetheless it gave him some clarity and peace in the end.

There was another fire, where his own home burned down. That was another pivotal moment for me as well.

Identifying with Batman gave me solace in the beginning. It gave me an emotional armor to deal with the fears and to manage my bats. In my early teens, I got beat up and punished for no reason and those experiences were life-shaping.

When I switched on this virtual suit of mine, this attire of safety, I found myself standing taller.

I found myself putting on a persona that was bolder, and I wouldn't know how to do it otherwise. The virtual Batman suit lent a level of bravado in my life.

As kids, especially when we're thirsty for love or recognition, to be embraced or accepted, it requires a system or mechanism to deal with those kinds of feelings.

When we find a system that works, we tend to latch onto it. When you put on an alter ego, and it seems to work, you don't let it go. It gave me promise and a way to move forward, a form of identity and strength.

The darkness came when I got home. There seemed to be little empathy for what I was going through. At that age, I didn't really know what empathy meant, but I knew I was starving for something, and that something was acceptance. Batman is an image of strength, but that doesn't mean there aren't weak moments in his life. Suppression takes energy.

Fear is exhausting.

If you are in a state of fear for a good part of a day and you go to bed exhausted, something gives. At times, I would cry. Batman probably cried too.

It's like a nerve center that has been overstretched in your body. When you try to fall asleep, to reflect and relax, the nerves snap. Then you snap. I was punished for crying because my dad thought it wasn't a manly thing to do.

If he heard me whimper, sniffle, or cry, he would come into my room to straighten me up. So I tried to make sure it didn't happen often.

During this chapter of my life, I often lurked. I had the ability to blend in, or at least to step back into the shadows. I wasn't the center of attention.

I wasn't the loudest in the classroom. I was trying to avoid eye contact. I was trying to blend in. For me, blending in was part of being stealthy.

I started developing my toolset for mirroring people. I found ways to fit in and the toolset got stronger as I got older.

A victorious moment for me was when I punched the ringleader of the bullies. He was kneeling down on the pavement, tying his shoelaces. I walked up to him and sucker-punched him right in the nose.

It was an emotionally satisfying moment. I didn't run, I stood there waiting for him to punch me back but he didn't.

There was a tiny little opening in the cloudy sky that day, it seemed like a beam of light came through and shone on me as I punched him. I felt glorious, my actions felt justified, and I found power in what I did. It changed the course of my relationship with the bully.

There's something stupidly animalistic in boys that makes us feel an innate need to mark our territory or to protect our space.

When I did this by punching him, I think it set him back. It made him realize, 'Hey, he's got something in him, so I'm not going to mess with him as much anymore.'

The bullying stopped and we became the best of friends over time. Weird.

Fear of Failure

Being invested in the protection and stealthiness of yourself is the result of a vision for yourself.

Mine was to become accepted, to become like the rest, and to become white.

There was no room for failure in that vision. I couldn't fathom it, I didn't want it, and I couldn't afford it. All I wanted was to be accepted. I could have reverted to being an introvert, but I knew that I had to put myself out there if I wanted to do the things I was interested in like playing sports. If I wanted to play sports, I couldn't do it alone. That's just a small part of what drove me, but there were never any thoughts of failure. I may have failed in my attempts, obviously.

Batman doesn't kill or imprison the Joker on the first try. Actually, the Joker finds himself even more emboldened because of Batman's failure. Perhaps my attempts to be accepted were viewed as a failure, but I didn't think about them as such.

If there was any failure during the day, it was squelched until I could reflect on it at night at home. It was not an ego thing, it was a protective thing, a survival thing. I still had my vision that I was working towards which meant I hadn't given up. I hadn't failed.

Shield to Protect

The Dark Side Batman series featured a particular, special suit that really resonated with me.

It was a suit I would intentionally wear because I needed to go solve something for myself or seek out a specific problem.

It was a suit that I would deliberately put on for a challenge that I had to deal with. In my mind at the time, the suit felt like I was in a clear bubble that was impenetrable.

It prevented people from getting close to me.

I feared getting hurt.

The bubble gave me extra awareness of the people around me. There were only certain times and certain people, like my teacher, that I would allow to come into the bubble with me.

I kept that bubble around me at all times, even with my own parents.

I can only imagine what my parents felt or thought of me at the time.

The bubble was my shield. It was my Batman suit. It kept that distance, physically and emotionally.

When I knew it was somebody I trusted, my body would relax, and they could come into the bubble. I would be less on guard because I felt a level of comfort.

The bubble only grew over time, and soon I found myself creating a mental castle. I built a moat around my castle, only letting the bridge down to those I wanted to bring in, as I have explained in earlier chapters.

In the castle, I organized my emotions into rooms and I would visit them constantly, knowing how to navigate them. The compartmentalization helped me put my fears aside and allowed me not to dwell on them. I couldn't constantly be bound by them, so I made sure I wasn't.

I think everyone does this in some way.

We all have our methods in how we deal with our fears. I think we all suffer from wanting to pursue a dream but are slowed, squelched, or hampered in reaching it because of our fears. They have control over us, and we don't have control over them.

Retooling the Arsenal

My arsenal was not what you would envision. Batman would have these little blades that he would throw, his 'batarangs', but my tools weren't violent in any way.

My arsenal had more to do with acclimation, tools I needed to adapt to the situation.

We are very impressionable as kids, what seems to work sticks with us.

One tool I used to blend in, as I have mentioned before, was changing the way I dressed. Another, as I wrote, was changing the way I smelled. I read at some point that the aroma of Indian food can seep through the skin, so I didn't want to eat Indian food and have my smell associated with my culture. Instead of eating what my mom prepared, I would cook my own meals. This is how ridiculous it was.

These intentionally created, combined characteristics were my arsenal. How I spoke, smelled, looked, smiled, dressed, styled my hair, everything was intentional.

I was mirroring my surroundings and I could deploy various tools from my toolset depending on what context I was in. There were different kinds of tools. Some helped me adjust myself to the situation, others helped me observe and understand my surroundings. All to just fit in.

When I was around 14 or 15, I was more introverted but very observant. I learned that I had to develop an empowering set of tools, my own arsenal, which would help me change myself and fit in.

Later, around 19, I had my first job, and I could afford to experiment. I now had the means to work on my style. I learned how to cook my own meals. I practiced with a microphone until I eradicated any hint of my accent.

I was grateful that at least I had a Christian, British name, Fowler, and the first name Steve. I thought, 'Thank goodness I'm not Rajesh Gupta or something like that. Oh my goodness, what would I have done?' I was grateful for a name that made it easier to blend in and I leveraged it as well.

Sometimes I catch myself still using these tools. There are some residual old habits. I still find it hard to look at myself in the mirror, but I'm much easier on myself than I ever have been. That only started about three or four years ago.

I found a way of being okay with who I am.

Showcasing Power

I didn't have the time to gradually change or accept who I was on a daily basis. I was not accepting myself for who I was, so I had to accelerate what I thought others wanted to see in me. I thought that it was necessary for survival at the time.

Being stealthy allowed me to take on a personality quickly. That was the key. It gave me a little bit of confidence, especially when I would perceive a different reaction from somebody after I changed something. I remember my dad saying, "Never look a white woman in the eyes." When I asked why, he said, "You'll never understand what their intentions are, especially if you're attracted to them."

So, I never did.

If they spoke with me, I would look down or I would intentionally pretend I was looking at them. I'd look at her forehead, or I'd look at her chin, but never in her eyes. As a result of that, I never asked anybody out.

I'd only accept if it was the girl that asked me out.

Ironically, after that, even though I'm aware there are beautiful women in my own race and every race, I've never been attracted to any other type of woman except white women.

I think I like white women because it was a challenge. Wondering how to ease into looking into their eyes became a challenge all of a sudden. That was the full extent of my promiscuity.

I felt that I was more accepted by girls and women than I was by men in those early years. I was validated by the way I suddenly changed because I would get the attention of the girls a little bit differently. I thought it was a way to inch forward. If the girl I was attracted to noticed the change, maybe others would notice as well. I would gain confidence that I could then build on, and that confidence was a form of power.

This power led to the pinnacle moment of sucker-punching a bully. It was like the energy stored up in every atom spilled out of my knuckles when I punched my bully in the face. It was like a Thor moment, where he throws a hammer at somebody and the world explodes. It was monumental for me. For me to get to that point, I had to burst through my bubble.

The amount of negative attention I had received began to decrease, whether due to time or the changes I was putting in, and I continued to be emboldened. I was able to blend in, I was able to acclimate, I was able to sound like others, and even smell like them.

I could maneuver through a crowd of people without anyone knowing it was a conscious effort. I fit in and therefore drew less and less attention over time.

It proved that my Batman suit, if you will, my stealthiness, was working. The metaphor of Batman gave me solace and perspective, and it made me reflective.

However, the reality was that my suit wasn't flawless. Tuning observational skills at a young age can lead to them being malformed, as our wisdom is limited when we are children.

When you don't have the proper guidance, you tend to hang on to certain observational skills because those seem to have generally worked. Those generalizations can lead to a lot of terrible things, such as bigotry.

People convince themselves of false beliefs, biases, and other falsehoods that don't benefit them. They waste time.

I found later that I had wasted my time and wasted some real relationships. I could have met and developed relationships with great people and learned so much more if I had just let them into my bubble.

I could've even eradicated my bubble because I didn't really need it, but I didn't question it. I relied on it because it worked when I was young. Approval and acceptance were the most important things to me.

Even when it came to professional settings, I saw it as a battlefield where I fought to make my parents proud. I needed to prove to them that I could be successful even though I didn't go to medical school like they desired.

Asian parents tend to have this idea that education means everything, that certain professions mean every-thing, and that you have to follow that way of thinking for the rest of your life. Nothing else matters. For them, that way of thinking is derived from wanting to survive.

My parents weren't rich growing up. They struggled. They came from very impoverished backgrounds, so that line of thinking became very ingrained in them.

It was always a promise of wealth they failed to reach and the idea that the next generation would be able to become rich. I inherited that way of thinking.

It was their own arsenal that helped them fit in, so they felt a sense of duty to teach their kids the same method of survival.

Understanding that now, I feel that I wasted so much energy on them because of my fears and my biases. It made it more complicated for me to have room to explore and find myself.

The hardest part is asking myself, 'Did any of those behaviors or my attributes of stealthiness, my Batman suit, affect my daughters?' I worry about that because I don't want them to ever have to pull out the suit. I want them to be themselves.

I want them to enjoy and explore their youth. I want

them to hone in on things that are joyous, not things that are always about protecting themselves.

I want them to feel safe. Looking back, the need to be stealthy took away my childhood. I think most boys dream of riding their bikes really fast, imagining that they're Superman with the wind in their hair. They want to play football on the field, act silly, and just be kids.

I missed out on all of that. I was more consumed by wanting to be accepted than being a child.

My concentration on trying to build a Batman suit, or be stealthy, took away some of those fundamental, foundational experiences.

If you have kids, let them play.

They may try to change themselves enough to be 'respectable', but they will lose the essential part of themselves that just needs to play.

We all need to play.

Chapter 5

DISRUPTION

There are two facets to disruption: personal and purposeful, the internal and external. I needed to start disrupting my old methodologies by resetting myself. I needed to stop overthinking. I needed to revisit my beliefs and value systems, my core principles, and how I operated.

I relied so heavily on these negative, and sometimes, false beliefs and biases based on my fears and experiences of my past.

I think that was the most disruptive for me because I was looking for more effective and efficient ways to influence people to take action on things that I needed to get done.

The disruption had to start with me internally.

I looked at myself differently and it took the patience of various people to help me recognize that I needed to stop overthinking.

It was a running theme for several years; I would pause and wonder what others were talking about. I had no understanding or realization that I was overthinking because I automatically would analyze situations that were based on my actions. I saw it as a kind of failure.

The disruption of myself began with the people who supported me. I became excellent friends with a senior director of recruiting in the company and she was a silent supporter.

When I would get on stage or I would get on a virtual meeting with my entire team, she would join. I wouldn't even invite her, but she would still join. She would provide feedback that would kindly and gently coax me to take advantage of opportunities to improve my narrative. Especially if I gave a presentation where I would discuss a particular point in too much detail.

I was overthinking and allowing less autonomy to others, allowing less of their own thoughts. I was leading people to what I wanted them to do, as opposed to influencing the result.

Her ability to share with me and give me that feedback was so kind and tender. It was subtle, and it took months for it to sink in.

She told me, "Look, you just need to stop and reflect on what you are going to think about and what you are going to present, and what you are going to think about needs to slow down. You need to be mindful of what others might be thinking, feeling, or considering."

All of this just led me to rethink and reprocess how I reflected on my behaviors and meetings, and also my behavior toward my team. This all helped, but I think the true disruption began when I turned 51.

As I wrote earlier in the book, it's like the children's story, 'If You Give a Mouse A Cookie'. The cookie is treated as a negative thing. It is like being rewarded for bad behavior.

A mouse is just going to chase the cookie and want more, and maybe even some milk.

For me, this meant being rewarded for achieving results by whatever means possible.

Everyone around me was less concerned about me and my effectiveness. It was not until a friend came and recognized my thought patterns and how I presented my body language. She observed me more intimately than anybody else had ever done. Her name was Vanessa.

At Microsoft, you are rewarded for results, which you are expected to achieve through any means necessary. If you followed the pattern of the most successful people at Microsoft, you would recognize a level of assertiveness that was out of the ordinary.

Taking a step back and seeing their behavior, it was very bully-like, where there were rewards for being an asshole. I just assumed that everywhere was this way because I spent so many years in that environment.

I thought that everywhere measured success in the way that I was being measured at Microsoft, that everyone was being rewarded for these kinds of behaviors.

I felt validated by reading the biographies of people like Steve Jobs, Bill Gates, and Jack Welch, who I now completely despise for the way they treated people in their organizations.

Even when they are talked about in negative ways, there is an overtone of admiration, of how successful they were, and the feats they have conquered.

These things moved the needle in technology, which enabled the society we have today. Even stories that came later, like Mark Zuckerberg, followed the same path, so I wanted to model myself in that way.

At Disney, it was a real awakening when I realized that not all people were driven in the same way. Not all people responded to the same level of instruction or behaviors that I exuded.

I was not given good feedback, but rather very passive one, and it was a low point for me. I thought, 'What am I doing wrong to influence these people to do what I need to do?'

I thought my old behaviors would just continue to work. When you are interviewed and brought into a company, they do not ask if you are an asshole.

They just assume you will get things done because that is what you claim in your resume and in your vernacular when you are describing yourself. In the interview, there is a process of bragging about the results that you can achieve.

This is what causes people to bring you into their companies. They gauge you on personality traits that are superficial at the moment you are interviewing.

When you are in the interview, you have your best face on. You are smiling, trying to form a connection, and that connection exudes some level of trust.

This trust is like the chrome of a bumper that conceals the rust or the rottenness of everything else behind it. It gets you the results that are needed.

This was a realization for me. I felt exposed. I had a perfect coat of paint on my body at Microsoft, but some people were now stripping it away.

My success at Disney was partial, and not nearly as prolific as it was at Microsoft. I did not realize that this had a lot to do with working with a set of creatives that I could not work with so productively.

I had to think differently, and I had to change who I was. I also had to realize who I was.

There was a person that I met there who tried to coax me into rethinking who I was. He also came from a very aggressive environment, similar to Microsoft. He recognized these patterns because he also shared them, but he had more of a looseness about him.

He was more relaxed and chill than I was. I was never able to convey chill in a tone that I would use. On the inside, I think that I was frustrated, anxious, and just wanted to get things done. This was exuded in my body language.

I think people around me recognized my struggle, pain, and anxiety. When you are that anxious, people tend to stay away from you. My ability to influence was more about me being more assertive in an asshole way as opposed to being kind and considerate. Disney became an awakening.

It could be a midlife crisis, but a lot has changed for me now. I focus more on writing, riding motorcycles, and photography. I have turned to more creative spaces in my life.

I think a midlife crisis is like having a moment of self-realization, where you want to explore something new. There is another aspect to that question. That is, as we get older, there is something in our subconscious that says, 'I want to learn more about myself, or I want to learn more about the world.

I want to learn more about my environment. I want to learn more about the things that I took for granted as a younger person.' I became a ferocious reader.

Some of the books that I have read have been hokey, some valuable, and some have truly given me perspective, but I am on this pursuit of knowledge like never before.

I think that this is a midlife crisis. It is the feeling of wanting to experience more. You want to experience more than you ever knew was possible as a younger person.

I think it has to start with the mind. If your mind is clear, you open up room for other experiences and you seek them out. The midlife crisis should not be considered a negative thing.

This type of disruption had me revisiting my fears and my biases. It put more emphasis on the things I needed to care about for myself.

I realized then that I needed to care more for myself than I did for the man, the boss, or the company.

I realized that these men were only happy that I was molded to their image. I was seeking to be successful based on a set of false perceptions.

What success meant for say, Bob Iger, the CEO of Disney, did not necessarily mean success for me. I fashioned myself after these leaders when I did not have any connection with them.

I didn't realize that this lack of connection with them was superficial, or that it was a fantasy that I had imagined that led me to pursue success.

The disruption was to try to sever that fantasy, to delineate what was real in me. I focused inward and asked myself what I was doing to cause this.

I took tidbits of information from people to get to a spot of realization. The realization that I was overthinking and had some negative beliefs and biases that were based on many of my childhood fears.

I am not claiming to be a psychotherapist, but there is one thing I believe to be true, and that is we as human beings are shaped almost fully by our subconscious and biases by the time we hit the ages of 11 to 13.

You are so impressionable at that time. Everything that happens to us within that time frame, give or take a few years, is taken right to the grave.

Everything there is potentially going to take us down a path, maybe one that is destructive, determined, detrimental, or for some, positive.

I took a detrimental path because I was living a falsehood. I was living a life that was not true to me.

I did not realize how exhausting it was until I reflected upon this time.

I am not saying that all of those experiences were bad. I think some of those experiences led me to be who I am.

I am grateful for some of those experiences because they taught me how to think differently. They taught me to make decisions that were more constructive than destructive.

I could have easily taken a destructive path during those times I experienced racism in my life. I could have hated all white people after that.

During those times, I turned on myself instead. Even as

I was growing up, in my career, or my early years at Microsoft, I was reflecting on what I could do better.

I was a perfectionist, looking to be that perfect employee. I was trying to be a guy that I could never really become.

Realizing that many years later highlighted some of the other negative qualities or spaces that I was in. These qualities and spaces caused me to overthink and behave in certain ways that were not necessarily conducive to well-being or to a place where everyone could be themselves.

All I can say from where I'm sitting today, in my mid-life crisis is: be yourself and do the things that you love and cater to your values rather than someone else's.

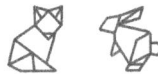

At first, I did not want to change myself. I did not want to disrupt my rhythm because it was working.

Then I got to Disney and it was not working the way I expected either. I resisted the self-disruption heavily and I was in a funky space during that time. We all associate the word stress in different ways and we all have different stressors. We are not always conscious of what triggers stress.

Subtle stress is an undercurrent that drives you nuts and can't always be explained but it affects you so much to the point that it affects your relationships around you.

It was frustrating because I could not share what was affecting me; I couldn't understand it. This is the beauty of being human. When you allow yourself to be vulnerable to certain people, you create a certain connection with them and you don't have to spell out what is causing stress.

They can interpret it for you, and it gives you further avenues to explore yourself a little bit more.

It is because of those formed connections that allowed me to open up a little more incrementally, slowly, and with kindness from someone else.

You can choose to either accept their kindness or not. When I did, I was so desperate to find myself, it was almost liberating when I was able to finally share my vulnerabilities.

Yes, I have read books that tell you that vulnerability is a good thing, but I have also been taught to shut my tears down. If I wanted to cry, or if I felt a strong emotion, I was told to shut it down.

What do generations of men like me do when they have been taught by their dads to not cry?

Well, you have to let it out somehow. Emotions must be let out through other means. You become an asshole, or maybe someone that you don't intend to be, but you have to let it out.

It's exuded in different ways. We may overeat, or over-drink, or do something else that makes us feel better.

It comes out in weird and unexpected ways, and if you do not acknowledge it, if you do not appreciate the disruption, that is when you know that you have lost.

When you do appreciate that disruption, you know that you are in a moment when you know you are about to experience an epiphany.

It is a pinnacle moment of gain that runs through every cell in your body and changes the state of your body.

Every one of your cells comes to a pause and doesn't move. It is a moment like, 'Something just happened here, and we are going to listen to what the electrons are going to tell us to do next, which is chill out.

Read about yourself, think about yourself, think about what you care about, and make that your priority.'

This was the disruption.

It took me years to truly reset.

I did not believe in certain methods of resetting. I was raised in a religious family who are still very religious, and as a result, I viewed everything that was some-what spiritual, even something like meditation, as hippie shit.

However, I tried meditation for two weeks and I did free-form journaling right after I meditated, where I just dumped my thoughts onto paper. This helped me to reset.

After just two weeks of journaling, my brain was slowing down. I was overthinking less, and I was moving into a space where I was much more mindful of myself and what I was doing. Before, it was just about projecting, but now it was more thoughtful, 'Hey, I need to see what I am projecting. I am about to say something. What is that I am about to say? Could I say it differently?'

I started to become more aware of myself and even more so coupled with meditation. That is when the real change happened.

I started reading about Buddhism, especially given that it had its roots in India and from the Hindu faith. I only started to read more about Buddhism because I wanted to see how different it was. However, it began to add to my disruption, meaning that I had to find calmness. I had to find the source of my pain and then deal with it.

That is the crux of Buddhism. It is where you find your inner peace, by finding the things that affect you negatively.

This eventually led me to the concept of something that I thought was never really fathomable. I realized you are the creator of yourself and you are in charge of creating your own experiences. You can create what you want.

This all came later. When you get into these modes of thought and internal deliberation, you come out thinking, 'Whoa, that was not so different, this was you all along.' This was just in my head. It helped me find out that having clarity and being deliberate about disrupting my old ways of doing things was the beginning of my new ways.

I am still reflecting, and I do not think that the journey of reflecting ever truly ends. When you can see yourself with more clarity, you are able to launch yourself more thoughtfully and purposefully. When you prioritize your values, you are also prioritizing what makes you happy internally and what makes you less stressed. This is not intended to sound narcissistic, but you have to learn to love yourself before you can love anyone else. This allowed me to love myself more than ever before.

My journey is not over.

I still cannot look at myself in the mirror, but I am working on it. I still have things that I need to do to figure out how to get beyond some of my old biases and fears.

The journey that I began, where I started to reflect, is where I was able to see myself for the very first time in a renewed way. This launched me into a less desperate and more deliberate state. Reflection was key.

When I started, I asked myself how I would see myself fitting in amongst the rest of the world. There are seven billion people on the planet and who is Steve Fowler?

Who cares?

I have space and I have something to give back. I feel like I have a purpose. If my world is just my two daughters and my family, great, that is all I need.

When I first took on this global view, I had a spiritual moment. When you look at the world and how the world works, especially from a human perspective, you realize that we cannot live this life unless we are all connected in some way.

This is grounded in reality, with the science behind it. We are connected to everything. We are connected to the trees, grass, bugs, earthworms, birds, and every animal and creature whether we like it or not, including humans.

We are connected, and it has all built this experience for me. Realizing this global experience has helped me understand my responsibility to others.

What do I give back that helps create harmony on this planet?

If I were to continue the way I had been, I would not be facilitating harmony.

I was creating space around me that didn't allow me to create the connections I so desperately wanted.

It was the realization of sharing my vulnerabilities, of trusting and allowing the drawbridge to drop from my castle over the moat.

I realized that maybe destroying my castle and just living amongst the people was what I needed to do.

It was envisioning what I had to have.

I had to go through the layers of protection and think about why I had this castle in the first place.

Why do I have to have this moat around this castle?

Why do I need to drop the drawbridge every once in a while?

Why can't I just leave this bridge down and let people come in whenever they need to?

Why did I create a bubble around me?

Why do I have an adverse reaction to white men who wear big belt buckles and cowboy hats?

Why can't I look at them as just another person who has their own fears and challenges, knowing they also want to connect but don't know how?

They are responding to me, perhaps, in their fears of what they don't know. Realizing what we don't know and what we fear because of what we don't know, is the gap in which change occurs.

My breaking point was at Disney in 2011 when I was working with both creative and technical people. I was not as validated in my skills of product knowledge, aligning goals, and getting things done as I had been at Microsoft. It was a self-evaluating moment.

I was not having nearly the impact I used to have at Microsoft, and I questioned just about everything as a result.

My pursuit of mirroring leaders like Bill Gates or Steve Jobs was the underpinning of my fascination with them and their ability to influence me.

The word 'influence' bothered me because I just didn't understand why I was not able to influence people of that magnitude. I was always focused on this magnificent problem or way of influencing.

I just wanted to exude influence. It was such a false, presumptuous space and I created a negative space for myself where I was relentlessly pursuing something that was right in front of me.

I didn't realize it. The disruption came as I started to reflect on myself and why I was not making the impact at Disney as I was in my previous roles at Microsoft.

The catalyst for that was very obvious but I did not realize that I was exuding what I was at Microsoft at Disney.

I was displaying brash and ego-driven behavior at Disney, people there just didn't work in that way. They wanted a way of thinking creatively. I could not bridge the gap between making logical decisions quickly, which I thought were necessary, versus leading creative people towards a decision that was opposite to what I thought my engineering teams should be executing. This was an awakening moment.

There was an HR person who was a very willing partner at the time. She had a personality of gold and saw joy in everything. She supported me in the organization of all of my needs, including dealing with negative attrition, people issues, and complaints.

It included recognizing my struggle amid the escalating amount of people wanting to understand me better. She was one of the first to help me recognize the differences in thinking and action.

One conversation took place in Kelowna, British Columbia, during our standard one-on-one meetings.

She asked me how I was doing, it was a moment of vulnerability where I finally admitted that I was not making the impact I felt I needed to make.

It was frustrating because I was not seeing progress and I was also not able to deliver on some of the commitments I had made. It became very obvious that I needed to do something different.

Lamenting with her helped me recognize that I had created this role for myself with the same assumptions that I had had at Microsoft. Here, I had to reset and take inventory of the organization, the culture, and their needs. I was so focused on the wrong set of needs, and, perhaps, even the wrong means to the end. I was trying to deliver more quickly than the organization could understand.

They could not understand me because I was so determined to be brash. I did soften, but not enough.

A key message from her was that I wasn't listening.

She walked me through a set of objectives to focus on that were more personal than anything else.

The people in HR just wanted me to listen. I was so determined to meet our goals and timelines that I was not listening.

My direct reports seemed to understand my drive, but they did not understand how to get to the end goal.

I was not willing to listen to their problems and the struggles they were encountering to get from point A to point B.

I was not bridging the gap between the old way of doing things and the new way of doing things very well either. As a result, I did not show much compassion.

The ultimate epiphany I had after leaving Disney was that compassion through active listening is crucial.

Reset

It was a long journey that led me to connect with an executive coach. I hired her as my coach for a time, relying on her expertise to help me get to a place where I could understand myself a little bit better.

I struggled for a few years. I would test concepts, meaning how well I was being received, at my next company. I had a bigger team than I did at Disney and the culture was somewhere in between Microsoft and Disney. I was able to make the impact I needed because I had the support of a CTO who understood engineering culture, as well as my drive. Some people needed to transform and transition from the old way of doing things to a more modern way of doing things.

I had Vanessa there, who was responsible for hiring me, but who also became responsible for hiring for my team's needs and upscaling talent.

She attended a lot of my meetings, listened to me and my narrative, and sat down with me after them. She would coax me into thinking, or at least questioning, what I was intending.

This gave me a fertile place where I could think differently. She was so gentle in the way she approached reflective moments for me.

She helped me realize how much of a perfectionist I was attempting to be and how that perfectionism got in the way. This led me to understand that I was overthinking quite a bit but also helped me understand why I was overthinking and how to set a direction more mindfully.

I needed to reset because I just did not feel that I was able to influence the kinds of changes I needed. I could see micro-changes, but I could not see the macro-changes.

I did not gain the macro-changes I was hoping for, so I just attributed it to the word 'influence'. I felt that I didn't have it, so I went down another negative path where I started to criticize myself in terms of presentation and leadership.

Although I was not willing to give up on my leadership roles or responsibilities, I was trying to pursue an answer as to why I could not influence.

Reflect

All the people who helped me were joyful, encouraging, supportive, but never critical.

They seemed to understand my struggle and gave me a few anecdotes that bolstered my overall self-confidence. I took their advice because I admired their skill in calming me.

I should have thanked them, but I didn't at the time. In hindsight, I realize that they helped tremendously in pushing me to reflect on myself.

When I started to reflect on myself, it was more through an understanding of my own set of values as opposed to corporate values.

I started to reset because all the coaching advice that I had gotten in the past, whether formal or informal, seemed to be aligned with the company and did not necessarily resonate with me. It was like trying to live in a place that is not your own home.

I think we all are creatures of comfort. In my brain, I sit on my beanbag and sip on a glass of wine. It is a silly metaphor, but to me, that is home.

When I was pursuing my career, mentally I was pretending to be in a home where I was sitting on a bar stool, sipping on a glass of wine, imagining, or at least pretending, to be comfortable.

When you are not comfortable, it takes you away from really having an engaging conversation or appreciating the person you are sitting next to.

You cannot sit for hours, and therefore, it changes how you listen and even affects your body language. You certainly become less compassionate because you are thinking about yourself.

Some people reach a later midlife leadership crisis, a plateau, where they can't seem to figure out how to continue growing and enhancing their growth.

What worked for them as an early manager or leader no longer does. They find themselves designated as a leader because they solve certain problems or issues in the organization and others like their ethos or the environments they created. They were rewarded and recognized because they were productive or enhanced the business in some way. They took on more responsibilities, learned how to deal with them, and applied similar rules to managing larger and larger teams.

Eventually, they reach a level where more is expected from them. They take the same approach, thinking that what has worked for them in the past will work now.

It is like raising your voice. You think that when you raise your voice at your wife or your kids, they are going to listen and do something.

Raising their voice will not be effective because they might be dealing with mid-level or even early managers who do not have similar experiences, beliefs, biases, or patterns of growth.

They reach a point where they wonder why you are not able to make the progress they once did as a leader.

This is where the mental plateau and struggle is reached. They seem to be working harder than they should, but they don't know why. They don't think to look to the past and reflect on themselves in order to change and move forward.

Sometimes, corporations may recognize this plateau and give a coach to help, but if the coach isn't actively listened to, progress will not be made.

The corporation may feel good that they are doing things to support their workers, and the workers may feel good by taking part in these coaching events, but the changes that are needed are not actually being made.

The readers I am addressing are the ones who can't get out of this confused state and never grow even when they aspire to.

As soon as I learned how to reflect on myself and my values and change to be an active listener and more compassionate, my leadership abilities were able to expand and grow.

Exposed

I felt overly vulnerable, like I needed to protect myself but I didn't know how, and I certainly didn't want to exude too much vulnerability.

I was still admiring the leaders of my past. I had a fantasy of maintaining some level of stoicism.

I was still struggling to understand my own identity. I feared that I was not delivering what was expected of me due to the lack of progress in achieving my business goals and objectives.

It was not even about the speed of these objectives, but feeling exposed because I was not delivering the level of value that was expected.

I was successful at Microsoft. I rose in the ranks quickly, more than the average.

I was accustomed to recognition and growth, and I envisioned growth in everything I did.

A lack of growth, of not being as influential, of not delivering on the business objectives or the commitments I made, made me feel exposed. To fail was to be exposed.

The reason I was so fixated on growth had a lot to do with previous successes, even if perceived. I was extremely competitive and took steps to deliver results as quickly as possible.

I worked hard to get people aligned with my objectives and goals that had been set with my managers.

When I started at Microsoft, I was 29 or 30 years old. I set a goal of becoming a VP by the time I hit the age of 45. However, I did not achieve that goal.

Perhaps it was an entitlement, backed by the success I thought I was responsible for, but I had a natural expectation of growth and what should've been achieved by that point.

It was not until much later that I realized my shortcomings and shortfalls. I felt stalled and like I was no longer in control anymore. It helped me to realize that I did not need to control everything.

I was being driven by a perfectionist mindset and trying to achieve a certain level of expectations.

I did not realize yet that I was only chasing some falsehood of perfectionism.

Realization

Those who supported me and helped me to reflect became my informal allies and mentors.

They tried to help me see past myself.

My frustration with my perceived lack of results made me confide in only people in HR. Those conversations led me to reflective moments, and I realized that I needed to spend more time figuring out how to share my vulnerabilities with my direct reports so they could better help me.

My boss at Concur, Steve deRham, was my favorite manager. As I have mentioned earlier in the book, he was kind and gentle, but could also be assertive in very constructive ways. Once while I was up on stage, as I wrote about earlier, I was trying to warm up the crowd by telling jokes about myself.

I thought it was well-received, but I was not getting the amount of laughter that I was hoping for.

Steve, who was in the audience, later came up to me and said, "Stevie, you have to stop telling jokes, especially when they deprecate yourself."

I did not realize how strongly I was coming across.

It was these little drops of perspective here and there that helped me piece things together, and got me to a place where I valued self-reflection.

Most of my mentors did not get to see me at the finish line, but they were certainly the catalysts towards the steps I needed to take and the actions I needed to self-reflect further.

Years after working for Steve deRham, I met a colleague who was a kid at heart. He didn't have an alter-ego; he was the same at work, after work, and during the weekends. I admired that he had the same personality all of the time. I did not realize until then that I had a work personality and an everything-else personality.

We first interacted because we sometimes had to work together on product direction and decisions, customer objectives and complaints, and the expectations of our customers, but we became friendly.

When we sat down and had lunch, he talked about his struggles and journey. I always thought he didn't have any struggles, that he was just naturally happy-go-lucky. He had such an extremely friendly and humorous side about him that I never saw the pain he had been through. I never saw any of his struggles.

I realized that he was sharing a vulnerable moment about how he was struggling, but he didn't exude it on the surface. This made me realize that we are all alike in so many ways, and my struggles don't need to be as hard as I am making them out to be.

I asked him how he alleviated his struggles, and he pointed me to the executive coach, whom I mentioned earlier, who did some transformational executive coaching with me.

Sometimes, a coach is more than just a coach.

This coach evaluated my belief system, my biases, and my fears, as well as pointed me to books that I should be reading for guidance.

That is when I started to read more, and when I started to pay attention to my growth areas.

Opened Up

The need for disruption began with my need to understand why I was not succeeding or making as much of an impact as I had in the past.

I realized that the problem was me. I had to disrupt my old behavior to become a more natural leader and tap into my natural leadership skills.

In the past, I leaned on my bullheaded self, the one who walked around and said, "Let me see what you are doing. Give me your metrics. You are not meeting your goals, and we are going to make sure that you get to the goal that we need or set."

Instead, I learned that being compassionate and understanding of why they were struggling to succeed within my organization was important. The disruption was liberating.

I felt like I was inviting people to help with a situation, problem, or other need; not only for personal growth but also towards the objective.

Progress was being made. Conversations gained additional clarity and added an element of mindfulness to individuals and their specific needs.

Understanding their needs allowed me to not only be more resourceful, but to also share with them how I struggled in the same way.

I was more willing to be open to sharing more constructive means of overcoming obstacles or filling the gaps that were created in the past.

Relationships can be understood as being like a ball of yarn.

When a cat gets ahold of a ball of yarn, they will unravel it. That could be any kind of disruption that happens, for the sake of this metaphor.

When you try to roll the yarn back into a ball, it doesn't roll back into the perfect ball that it was when you started.

When you do not take the time to understand how it unraveled and how it got knotted, you cannot undo the knots.

That's why it's tricky to figure out how to fix the 'mess of yarn' of relationships at home or in the workplace … once things have already gone awry. But if you start with a 'common thread', so to speak, or in this case, I guess a common 'yarn', you can roll that ball back up in a smarter way.

Working together with a group in which everyone has a collective need, objective, or adverse situation acts as this common thread, lending a shared understanding that was not understood before.

Once you get to that level of understanding, you become more compassionate but still maintain focus and direction on where you need to go. Together, you can find alternatives to get to the ultimate objective.

It results in a much more mindful relationship than ever before.

Before my realization, I never had the compassion to listen, and therefore, I did not have the language to interact. I could not understand others.

I didn't even take the time to understand them. I thought that constant driving, raising my voice, and pushing harder was the solution.

Eventually, I began taking the time to actively listen to the challenges they were facing.

Whether it was personal, professional, or organizational, I realized that I could dig into my past and my wisdom.

I could share with others how I had personally overcome challenges, or just brainstorm through various challenges.

This gave them the space to lead, which is something every human wants to do. They want to lead themselves, they want autonomy, and I was not giving it to them before.

It was magical, and it actually became less exhausting for me because I no longer had to solve the problem.

Instead, I could distribute it. I could share it.

I could empathize.

I could take on a part of the problem, and relegate the rest to another person who was better at it than me. Recognizing these possibilities was very liberating, more than I had even realized.

What a fool I had been.

I still am a fool, but I like the kind of fool I am now because I am willing to be more vulnerable and share my failures, but still be working to overcome some of those failures.

To be foolish is so human-like, and it is a much better place to be than to pretend to not be a fool.

Foolishness allows me to be joyful in the moment. I don't have to be contrived. I don't have to be someone I am not.

I can just be my own kind of fool.

There are two forms of disruption: negative and positive disruptions.

The negative disruption happened due to my pursuit of some fantastical objectives, set of roles, and aspirations towards success.

They were based on falsehoods, certain beliefs, and biases. I was no better than a gerbil caged in a wheel, spinning faster in order to feel more productive, but just not getting anywhere.

The positive disruption happened when I got off of that wheel, and realized that what I was doing was trying to mirror people that I could not actually mirror.

It is liberating.

Chapter 6

IDOL

have always admired idols and their power to influence. In my case, idols of business, but I can understand how others look up to musicians or other world leaders.

Without having a true understanding of why Bill Gates or any of the other idols I had in my life had influence, I wanted to mimic and mirror them.

Their success allowed them to change the world in ways that were technology-driven, but also in a way that influenced society.

Their societal success left me in a state of awe, and I would hang onto their every word.

I wanted to influence others by mirroring their public personas. I thought having the same level of influence that they had would give me the validation that I was seeking.

However, the idols I was following weren't the people I imagined them to be.

Idols We Create

The people we attempt to mirror are often mirages created in our minds and not how they actually are.

We read about them and visualize their success.

The success that these idols have, whether it be monetary, or in leadership, is perceived. We do not know some of the challenges that these idols have had or have overcome in their lives.

I was so absorbed in Microsoft and general tech culture. I was part of the first generation of personal computing, software, and the early capacities of the internet. The leaders in our industry were moving and enhancing the capabilities of an individual.

In my youth, I had an Atari 800, a Commodore 64, a tape drive, and a modem. I thought that I had it all. Soon after that, the personal computer, the PC, was introduced.

Then, Microsoft came along and created the Microsoft Disk Operating System or DOS, and I got a bootlegged copy.

It allowed me to have a certain level of power and made me curious about Bill Gates and what he was doing in order to make this software.

I was enamored by the intellectual horsepower that goes into the creation of something like that. At that time, I was only about 17 or 18, and he was making it relatively affordable. How does someone make this product so affordable and accessible? I was fascinated by it.

One measure of Microsoft's success was their ability to hook me or anyone interested in computing or software, into their product. I was so immersed in software at that time.

I was not a super geek, but I was just geeky enough to be able to navigate my way through writing code and programming.

I soon became curious about different coding languages, computer architecture, and computer systems.

The way they interacted and collaborated was through software. I remember thinking, 'Wow, that is such a power to be able to influence me and give me the capability to navigate a device that allows people to use software that I wrote.'

I thought about how rewarding it must have been for the inventors, but again, I only saw what I wanted to see.

I idolized them, and this empowered me to be more successful. When I had time, I wanted to immerse myself in this world however I could.

I read their various biographies and was fascinated by every word that was written about them. This only made me worship them more.

They became these idols, in my mind, that I would bow to. I do not mean to make that sound religious, but it was a pseudo-religion I created in my mind that I was following.

Perceived Influence

The idols that I looked up to were easy for me to shadow and follow. I saw their level of success and wanted that for myself.

As a child, I idolized people and I attached myself to the concept of their influence, not knowing that what I saw was only my own perception of them.

I wanted to be a student of technology, so I absorbed everything I could from magazines and books. This further idolized these individuals through learning about the efforts and work that they put into their products.

It helped satisfy my curiosity about computer software. The people who I idolized became my teachers from a distance.

They were at the pinnacle of success and seemingly could have whatever they wanted: influence, power, riches, success, happiness, and joy.

In my family, you tended to fall on either the religious preacher side or on the medical side. I do not think that I have any member of my extended family who is also an engineer.

I had no one to lean on within the family, no one who supported my ambitions, so I had to find someone externally. Yet at that young age, I was afraid of seeking out any sort of informal or formal mentor.

I did not have much guidance in terms of career aspirations or success. I couldn't find it with the people in my life, so I turned to these virtualized leaders in the industry.

It became important to me because it became something I could attach myself to.

I wanted to steer myself toward a place of success as much as I could.

I wanted to guide myself under that influence. It may have been escapism. I was searching for my identity, latching on to anything I could identify with, and therefore made the leap to become one.

This gave me a symbolic yardstick of what I needed to incrementally grow. It gave me a virtual roadmap to what I thought would make me as successful as they were.

Much of it had to do with the fact I was seeking guidance. If you think about how fragile we are as young humans, how vulnerable we are, and how quickly we latch onto things that we admire, there exists a fine line. You may latch on to bad things and people or to something good or positive. There is also the possibility of latching to something extreme, like joining a cult.

We, as humans, all seek out someone who we can aspire to be.

I wanted the same success as my idols because of my insecurities about who I was.

I sought external factors to get over my lack of confidence.

I did not like who I was as a child, and I did not like the color of my skin. I had a hard time looking at myself in the mirror, even to this day, as I've noted. I was never believed to be someone that could do much.

In the game of life, I always felt like I was the last one picked to be on the team. When you feel that way, you try to make yourself more shiny.

I wanted to be the guy that was the first one picked.

When I started receiving validation for my work and for my success, I would do everything to build on it.

I was building towards success in the image of those I saw as most successful.

Clarity

I had a moment of clarity the day I realized I was trying to replace my own values with the perceived values of my idols. I had no idea that there was any power in the distinction between my values versus those of others.

I took the time to understand what triggered me and what it meant to me. I started to understand the root of my triggers, whether it be my fears, biases, or some artificial beliefs.

The act of idolizing someone else meant I was creating my beliefs off of a fantasized someone and how I imagined their values to be.

Now, if I look at Bill Gates or Steve Jobs, I see that they are just average humans. They just happened to be more driven or confident than others.

They believed in what they wanted to do and did what they needed to do.

They were not driven by money, they were driven by a solution that they needed to build.

Were they narcissists? Sure.

As I reflected on myself and my values, I realized that I do not think I am a narcissist. Narcissistic values are different from mine.

This is when I realized I was pretending to be someone who I am not. I am pretending to be a person who is self-violent, self-abusing, and lacking awareness. When I came to grasp all of these negative attributes, I realized that my mind was creating a person that was bigger than life itself.

I realized the power that I had to create my own experiences, as opposed to just following and shadowing somebody else's experiences.

Am I as driven as Steve Jobs and Bill Gates?

I would argue no. I do not have my own company. I am not known to the world as an innovator.

Am I holistically Steve Fowler now? Yes, absolutely.

This is where my clarity began to come.

It was the realization of my own personal values and what matters to me that keeps me calmer, less stressed, and less worried about perceived success or notoriety.

The power of influence that I was chasing was in front of me the whole time.

I'm intentionally working on influencing just one person a day. It is just about stopping and recognizing that I did in fact influence somebody.

It is knowing that I am both a student and a teacher at the same time, all the time.

If you shift your brain towards being a student more often than teaching, you will gain some clarity.

You learn how to be more curious and how to actively listen. There is a strange thing that happens when you actively listen and are compassionate to yourself. You become much more aware and more mindful.

You become adjusted to your heart's needs, and how your emotions connect to your brain. The left side of your brain and the right side of your brain join and wonderful things happen.

Reference Points

Having that moment of clarity, that realization that I was chasing someone else's values, was a pivotal moment in my life. That was when I started to study what I valued in myself.

These transitional points in time help you to admire what you have achieved but also to reflect on what you have yet to accomplish.

The distinction between idolization and worship is made clear when you can idolize a particular path that someone took without worshiping what they have done.

Their call to action will be much different than mine. My path to wisdom is certainly going to be different from theirs and I have to allow it so I can still lean on others. This is why reading is so valuable. Reading gives perspective and you gain anecdotes and wisdom from people that you can associate with and recognize.

The association with wisdom, or learning, is not about worship. It is more about the cognitive presence and gain of knowledge that adds to your own experience.

You are then able to experiment with what you have just learned, ponder upon it, and adjust accordingly. These affect us subconsciously, where we are not spending energy trying to be somebody else, but are trying to be more of our true selves. It's how our energy should be spent.

When you begin self-reflecting and you start to become more aware of yourself, you will know that you are on the right path.

I was captivated by certain concepts about myself that were lurking in my mind and learned it's important to take advantage of my closest friends.

These are the people who give unconditional support, and also gently give constructive criticism in a way that can be absorbed without feeling rejected or denigrated.

When you are willing to solicit feedback and share certain vulnerabilities, you will gain deeper levels of connection but you also gain validation.

This is the power of humans. When you establish these types of connections, you are able to grow together.

After all, we are social animals, and if we did not have that connection, we would not be able to grow.

My tool became to learn to ask better questions, to share my vulnerabilities, and to learn and develop trust with others.

This all starts with trusting yourself.

When you trust yourself, you can unravel things like personal beliefs and biases, question them, and then open the door to others to see if they believe in the same things you do.

There is a certain danger in power.

When you associate yourself with certain beliefs or people who lack critical thinking, you can get sucked into things that compromise what you actually want, be it certain churches, religions, or cults.

These things make you believe that just paying your tithe will bring about a solution to world hunger.

No, it is just going to go in someone's pocket. You have to apply your critical thinking to avoid these situations. If you want to do good work, you have the power to do so.

Good work will come with being validated and having good support around. You have to put your neck out there first, which is what I first had to learn how to do. It was an interesting journey for sure.

Being vulnerable is not easy.

Mentees

I do not know what the exact split is between being a teacher and being a student, but I do know I want to be more of a student than I am a teacher.

Teaching is not to be presumptuous that you know it all. Rather, it starts with teaching yourself.

If you take a complex concept like your own emotions and values and how they connect, you can teach yourself how to connect further.

Then, you are inviting yourself into a cycle of learning and teaching, learning and teaching.

As this happens, I think bystanders will accidentally learn from you too. This is where the awareness of teaching comes from. You may be teaching somebody at any time, whether through an influential act or others seeing what you have done. It could be a learning opportunity for them.

This is the danger of being a leader and being a public figure. Even for the idols, they have to be vigilant about how they are perceived.

I am not saying that I have to be super vigilant because I do not need to have a PR person. I do not even have a digital presence. I am fairly obscure in terms of the artificial audiences out there. I love being in the audience of my friends, but I am not the one up on stage.

I like to be in the mix, meaning sharing thoughts, laughing joyfully, sharing happy moments, being critical in constructive ways, and being a part of society in general. I think we all like to do this. We learn from each other and think about how interesting it is to do so.

Negative or positive, we are still constantly learning. I think our knowledge is growing all the time. When we think we are just sharing, we are also teaching. It is not a formal exercise of being a student and teacher, but a more informal teacher and a student dynamic.

I love the idea of seeing ourselves as students again because it creates an openness, an open-mindedness, and an open-to-learning state, that allows us to expand our thinking.

We create new beliefs or even try to keep our beliefs in check, to be expanded and validated further.

Students can help others learn. To use a metaphor of an actual student, when homework is shared with the teacher, the teacher, because of their experience, understands the student's level of comprehension from the homework.

The teacher may be blown away or understand that the student has the general concepts, or they realize that the work is not up to standard.

The student is just not learning. They are not applying themselves. They are not listening in class despite me giving them all the clues.

A teacher is someone who might be more experienced in a particular area than you are. When you allow yourself to be a student, no matter the situation, you will learn how much expertise a particular teacher might have and what you can learn from them.

Those external measures influence our growth.

When I left Christianity, I didn't do it formally, I was still playing the role of a Christian. I was going to church, praying and asking for forgiveness on Sundays, but sinning the rest of the week. I was truly living a facade.

Maybe it makes us feel good that we can offload our sins to someone who we cannot see and then assume that all is forgotten and all is forgiven. The same principle continued for me as I tried to seek out an idol because I wanted my past to be forgiven.

I wanted my insecurities to be forgiven and I wanted to latch myself on to my hopes. I wanted something to help me overcome my fears, so I would attach myself to certain beliefs.

There are books written about attachment theory, which discuss how we attach ourselves unconditionally to our moms at an early age. When something happens, like physical or verbal abuse, we are pushed away from being naturally attached to our parents.

We try to find something else to augment our need for attachment, a sense of security, a comfort blanket of knowledge. This can come from idolization. This comfort blanket is woven by the threads of influence strung together by this individual.

There is a moment where a seed is planted in your head, a realization that, 'I can look at something objectively, and when I look, I can see all the layers of my curiosity, compassion, and emotional connection.

I see a set of experiences I want to experience myself, as opposed to trying to relive or idolize somebody else's experiences.'

If you continue to latch yourself to an idol in blind faith, no matter what it is, whether it's a rock star or a religious figure, you relinquish yourself to that idol.

You also do not know why you have relinquished yourself.

You almost enslave yourself to somebody else's ideals, beliefs, faith, or values.

When you follow someone so blindly, you are no longer as independent and are cautious about your beliefs and values. It is necessary to let go of leaning on others, and just hoping to ride somebody else's coattails.

We are as unique as handmade pottery. We are all shaped slightly differently, but if you took us at a birds-eye view, we all still look like a bunch of vases.

To get closer and be able to see and distinguish your markings, your lines, how you are made, and how you are a slightly different shape or volume from the other vases is pretty exciting.

When you see that you are unique, you start to build on it and leverage accordingly. You start to navigate outside a mass perspective that you felt obligated to belong to.

If you first start with belonging to yourself, you can then see which groups you want to attach yourself to with far more clarity. I think it enhances critical thinking because you will know with certainty what you want and need for yourself.

Don't sacrifice your values or what is right for you. When you start to gain clarity, you may even stop reading these self-help books because these self-help books tell you what you already know you should be doing.

Sometimes they are presenting the obvious and we just are too thick-headed to learn and believe too much in some other ideology.

Maybe we even idolize them and we do not necessarily know how to break down the value and meaning they provide to us.

Therefore, you will just remain unchanged because it is easier.

If you don't try to challenge yourself, you will never find a way to be challenged. This prevents you from actually reaching the levels of success that you want. You are an individual with a set of strengths that you can contribute, which are unique to only you.

You are much more powerful than you think you are.

Chapter 7

POWERS AND LIMITS

When I think about my love for the fictional figure of Batman, I always think about superheroes and their powers and limits. I actually love Batman and have always felt close to that figure because of his limits, as well as his powers. He is fully human, makes mistakes, and has weaknesses, just like me.

So let's think about powers and limits.

When facing limitations, when I am cornered by fear or some presumption of attack, I fall into the habit of trying to protect myself.

I try to be assertive, but I am limited to knowing the certainty or uncertainty of a specific environment.

This used to cause me to create a type of artificial power, which is one extreme end of the reaction spectrum.

On the opposite end, I now understand and I am in touch with, is my vulnerability. There have been different times, and maybe even varying levels of empowerment, when vulnerability has been shared or a connection arises, that creates more confidence.

Therefore, I felt a sense of belonging that brought more clarity, calmness, and joy.

The other end of that spectrum was exhausting. It was an anxiety-filled time spent on significant amounts of overthinking and wanting to be able to control all external factors. If there was such a thing as a tuning fork in this scenario, you would have to strike your fork and resonate with the frequency first.

You have to learn to listen to yourself and tune into yourself. Develop that bat hearing, so to speak, towards the resonance of yourself.

Confronting your limitations and power can lead to exhaustion, but also immense reward. It is exhausting in the sense of the amount of thought put into developing a false sense of power.

Earlier in this book, I wrote about how I gathered intelligence on people and my surroundings. The amount of effort that went into that was me trying to control external factors as opposed to understanding my fears and managing them accordingly.

I spent an exorbitant amount of time doing silly acts of intelligence gathering as opposed to just living in the moment. I could have been more cognizant of my objectives as opposed to the falsehoods and narratives I was creating in my mind.

Those fallacies were driving weird behaviors in me and I was overtaxed.

Absurdly at the time, I thought that it was the power that would be gained from what I had deemed successful but it also inadvertently created a barrier to achieving further success.

This cornered me into assuming various falsehoods around power, which assumed that I would overcome my limits through aggressive power posturing.

I spent more time reflecting on the situation as opposed to reflecting on my motives.

The external motives that shaped my perspective had to do with my subconscious need to overpower a situation. Overpowering meant that either I had to be an asshole or a bully, in the way that perhaps I had been bullied when I was a kid.

I wanted to fight fire with fire. I did not realize that I needed to take a step back, assess my internal fire, and apply the right tool instead of trying to use a hammer to put out a fire as opposed to using water.

I think the limitations I have now are more reflective and are from a place of learning.

I feel like I am learning more about myself. As a result of those learnings, I am discovering that my inner wisdom has more tools to control my emotions, reactions, and capabilities.

Today, I feel that this transformation is more empowering, not in an invasive way of power maneuvering, but more of an inclusive or collaborative enrichment in everything that I do, say, or work. It is empowering as opposed to overpowering.

Struggles

If situations were too perfect, we would never grow. As humans, we need to struggle in order to learn. You may think you're learning by reading or putting yourself into certain scenarios.

For example, in one extreme, you could belong to a cult. You join a cult and you think you've found your purpose.

Someone may give you the red pill to commit suicide versus the blue pill to discover your potential and knowledge, to connect with greater wisdom than ever before.

Without a sane and grounded approach to struggles, you will not be able to decipher one option from the other.

Humans are much like sheep, they want to follow. We love to be part of a bigger crowd. If we see a popular group going in a false direction, that is a struggle, especially if they are in too deep.

Conversely, you could go down the path of overlearning, which leads you to falsehoods of perfectionism, where you are trying to be a different person than you naturally are.

I think the struggle has to be natural. In some ways, it could be understood as a micro-dosing of yourself, where you learn a little bit about yourself at a time and incrementally move in that direction. This creates happiness and joy.

If you don't find happiness in the result, then you know you are backed into a corner that you should not be in.

I struggled because I did not want to swing the pendulum too far one way by heavily criticizing myself.

I appreciated criticism of myself, but not in a deprecating way.

I needed critical reflection in a more measured and open-minded way, which led me to be more mindful of myself.

Once I started being mindful of myself, I was able to practice being mindful of others. It changes the power dynamics.

You are not trying to control someone else, but you are doing more to control and manage yourself more mindfully and therefore being more mindful of others as well.

Reorient

There are so many lessons to learn about how you manage yourself. Challenge yourself to go through a journey of learning and understanding yourself. Learn from others, as well as from unexpected resources such as people you don't like. I am fascinated by understanding how my brain processes the effects of others on my emotions and how they play out.

Regardless of the left-brain/righ-brain concept and the expectations around the creative side versus the logical one, I think a better equilibrium is reached in our learnings about ourselves when we apply both.

Allow yourself to be creative, to be a kid again. The closest thing that we can associate creativity with is having a youthful curiosity.

When we lived in Afghanistan, I jumped off the second floor with a paper parachute that I had made out of construction paper.

I had seen my G.I. Joe successfully jump with a parachute made out of paper and I thought it could suspend me as well. So, with Scotch tape and paper wrapped around my waist, I jumped off the second floor.

My mom yelled at me for doing such a foolish thing, but I taught myself a lesson.

Later in life, everyone laughed at that moment of curiosity. Sure, I could have been hurt, but I also learned how to be more critical of my ideas.

You should not be jumping off second-story balconies with a paper parachute made out of Scotch tape and construction paper.

You need to apply some critical thinking. Sometimes, critical thinking only comes after you try something creative or stupid.

My mom would always wonder how little boys stayed alive because my sister never did anything dangerous.

I am truly surprised I survived some of the things I did.

Later, based on my understanding of my limits and power, I learned that I needed to calm down. In my mind, I had to take a break. I needed to stop because the madness that I was creating was becoming a compounding problem. It was leading to unhappiness and the moat around my castle was becoming bigger and deeper than I had needed in my life.

I did not necessarily see that at the initial onset. I thought my strategy would continue to work time and time, over and over again.

I started realizing that no one wanted to make a connection with me anymore. They were always artificial connections without any depth, except for a few people who believed in me. They were trying to build a bridge towards me and I would break it down, even destroy it marginally, inch by inch. I was pushing people away, creating a deeper moat. I was doing whatever it took to protect me in my castle.

I knew that I had to stop and get to a place where I understood myself. I had to learn about tools that allowed me to self-reflect.

These were simple things like meditation for five minutes a day, breathing exercises to calm my anxiety, or trying to focus on the moment.

When I go to work out now, I am intentionally working out and paying no mind to anything except for working out. It is about being intentional about my attention.

My inner self gave me more clarity and more calm in the connections I needed. Those needs first start by reflecting on yourself, knowing what you need, and creating a set of values that are true instead of delusional. Those delusional values are either inherited or adopted from others, where there is no depth in those values, you are just adhering to them because they are tied to a standard of previous success.

This standard was not yours, it was someone else's. When you believe in what you want and pursue something while acknowledging the fact that you are indeed fallible, knowing that you will learn from your faults and failures, you achieve the freedom and clarity you need to grow.

All of a sudden, admitting to these things is liberating, and it creates a stage for being more open-minded.

Equilibrium

I had to reset my scale when I stopped idolizing everyone else.

It is fine to idolize or admire, but let's transpose the idolizing to admiration. You can have admiration. You can admire your wife, your spouse, your partner, and your children. Those are very honest and legitimate admirations because there is something about them that you wished you had, or you just understood and can equate to your core self.

Admiring loved ones gives you meaning, gives you purpose, and an association and confirmation with your own set of values. It brings more joy and happiness as a result.

That is where the equilibrium is. You will always struggle, but life is filled with these opportunities.

You will question what you will learn, just as I question everything that I have learned. I continue to do so because, to some degree, all of us pursue the illusion of perfection.

We subconsciously know that perfection is an illusion, but we cannot give up the notion that the journey to perfection is filled with failure.

This does not necessarily mean that you will reach perfection, but it is a pursuit, and that pursuit means embracing failure along the way.

This is also an equilibrium.

Road Trip

There are some adages I would reconfigure, like 'Stop and smell the roses', to 'Stop and smell the roses, but pay attention to the rose. Be fully intentional about smelling the rose.

Do not just assume that this rose smells like the last rose you smelled. Take it in. Perhaps the white rose smells slightly different from the red rose.'

Take the example of a road trip. As children, we were excited about taking a road trip with our parents. Somewhere along the way, we lose interest in our parents and we lose interest in road trips.

We become self-centered and we pretend we know everything because that is what is expected of us.

This is the adolescent phase where we have gained just enough knowledge to feel smart, but we remain sophomoric, foolish, and undeterred by what we think to be correct.

We do not have compassion for what we have learned, nor do we have a true depth of knowledge. It is all transferred knowledge, or implied, as opposed to being ingrained or lived in.

As we get older on the road trip, we are grown up now, and we have learned to appreciate life in general. We appreciate not only the time with our parents but also the gift that time is.

We appreciate observing everything that is around, like

the seat in which we sit, or the window that we look out of. We appreciate the external environment, observing if it is a cool day or a warm day, and rolling down the window to feel the wind through our fingers with our arms out of the car. Those are all things that we start to not take for granted anymore.

Once you get to that point, you realize how little you know about the road trip, or where you are going, but you are still enjoying it.

Learning comes down to an understanding where you are cognizant of your growth and the stage you are in. You wonder about your levels of knowledge, from a topic, to someone else, to yourself.

You wonder about whether you are just parroting or mirroring somebody else, or if you're being authentic. It helps you realize whether you are ready or if you have more learning to do.

Mirroring is both a subconscious and conscious act that needs to be undertaken for us to learn to grow, or even move from one stage of growth to another.

Growth is the journey, it is the road trip.

It is the understanding that sometimes you do not always have to learn just about yourself, but about everything around you.

Stick your arm out the window and feel the wind. Do the air motion with your hands where you feel the air, like how dogs hang their heads out of the window of a car.

We all love the feeling and we have to appreciate that moment. That is what this journey is all about.

Framing

When I was younger, I would compartmentalize every-thing. I now know it was a coping mechanism. It allowed me to intentionally shut things off and focus on the things that I wanted to focus on.

Unfortunately, I leaned towards the things that gave me superficial powers, which produced a series of negative results and behaviors and diminished how much I would learn about myself or about a situation.

When I think about how I frame it today, I frame the lim-itations as opportunities. I ask what actions or steps I can take to overcome some of those limits.

Are the limits made up, based on somebody else's bias? No one ever told me to not jump off of the second floor with a construction paper and Scotch tape parachute, but I had either enough stupidity or courage to jump off anyway.

As a little boy, it hurt, but I thought that I was made out of rubber at 7, so I luckily didn't break anything, and instead just got up and looked for validation.

I looked at my mom and dad, the people around me, and said, "Wasn't that cool though? I built a parachute."

I did not think about any other negative attributes. I was just looking for validation. As I grew, the search for val-idation became less and less innocent.

It was more about my perceptions of what was safe and unsafe, how I needed to protect myself, and how I could be perceived as successful based on idols and their ideologies.

Framing limits is to understand your creative nature, and what you need in order to bring joy and happiness. Do not forget the left side of your brain, the logical side. You need to bring some logic, but the logic doesn't have to be binary. It doesn't have to be just a one and a zero, it can be a 0.1 and a 0, or 0.2 and a 1. It is more about how you apply your thoughts without being overly critical of yourself, allowing for creativity and also allowing for failure.

Jumping off the second floor could have resulted in far worse damage to me and I got lucky. I am not saying that everybody should jump off a second floor, but there is some level of taking risks and applying some critical thinking along the way.

My journey began with me wanting to fit in, and then learning about how to deal with adversities, as we all do.

Adversities are real, but at times are embellished in our minds. We take action to protect ourselves, to not only survive but to revel in a measure of success.

We build ourselves up and form methods or strategies to deal with everyday life.

We may lurk in the shadows where we can continue to be unseen, and continue to lurk in learning methods. These are only futile learnings because we have not addressed who we really are yet.

We have to be intentional about the disruption that we want to create.

Self-disruption is changing the way we think about ourselves, changing the way we engage with ourselves, and seeking our own values and needs for satisfaction.

Satisfaction has to be for the self. It has to start with you, which then leads you to a better understanding of your limits and also a better understanding of the power you want to gain for yourself.

For me, I want to do things that make me happy. I want to continue on a path that gives me the liberty to apply myself in the way I want to, which is to give.

I want to help others see how to also overcome some of their own challenges and perspectives, and get to a place where they are bringing their uniqueness to any challenge they may embark on, professionally or personally.

Throughout much of my life, I thought about power in many ways. The negative aspects of power had a lot to do with my confidence, my obsession, and the anxiety behind my obsession with influencing others.

This led me to falsehoods, false beliefs of myself, and false beliefs of others.

Now I frame power as a way to enrich. A path that leads to more confidence.

One of the key attributes of confidence is knowing what you want and knowing that you are happy and joyful in what you are doing.

That is pretty empowering. Now, I take the time to learn about myself as much as possible but without trying to be a recluse. The connection with others that you trust and value, who are equal to you and share your values, helps you to learn and enhances your growth and journey, potentially forever.

You are your best self when you understand yourself.

To know yourself is a lifelong journey. It has to involve reflection, experiences, and growth.

To get on the right path, you have to reflect. Spend time with your thoughts, and as I have said throughout this book, maybe even journal what tools you think you may have to understand how you think and your emotions.

It is being kind to yourself as well, and making sure that reactions are validated not only by yourself but shared with your closest friends and colleagues. You have to believe in a certain level of mindfulness. You have to develop a practice where you become significantly more aware of your inner self and internal state, which translates into the clarity of who you are.

Try new things, be creative, and take on new activities. This helped me discover and enjoy what I wanted. I needed to shape myself before I could even try to shape the surrounding things.

Part of this was shaping my self-perception. My self-perception was very scary. It was a 'scared Steve' versus a 'new Steve'.

> The past cannot be changed. What some would think and try to do is rehearse a future where they don't know what is going to happen or not. There is nothing negative about future planning, having ambition and goals, and being mindful.

Having the clarity you need about yourself is great, as well as trying new things. I think the key is to find your values and principles.

What are those guiding principles for yourself? How can you be more compassionate with yourself? It is about setting personal goals that help you understand your capabilities and asking yourself, 'What is important to me?'

Do not be afraid of counseling or therapy.

I think having those resources and taking advantage of them, even coaching or mentoring, is important for a working set of goals.

It helps you to understand your capabilities, and reflect on them, as well as your fears and vulnerabilities. Having counseling, therapy, mentors, or coaches can facilitate a much more structured path toward self-discovery.

It is also about reading and educating oneself. I am a non-fiction reader, so reading philosophy, psychology, and self-help books helped me to frame an understanding of myself.

Paired with some critical thinking, ask how it can apply to you, and make sure it can. Don't just read for the sake of reading and absorbing what somebody else says. It might work for the masses, but it may not work for you, so be cautious.

Having a mindfulness or meditation routine also helps you to be cognizant of what reduces your stress. I think there are also important health benefits from these practices, like getting the rest and exercise that you need. It will help you with clarity and with being mindful.

My journey through meditation and journaling gave me an intentional quiet time when I could reflect on myself. They are some of the greatest enablers of self-discovery.

To become better at knowing yourself, engage in self-reflection often, seek new experiences, and be open to feedback and personal growth.

Embrace both your limits and your powers.

CONCLUSION

When I look at myself in the mirror today, I see pride and joy and I attribute that to what I care for and who cares for me.

Through reflection and insights, I came out knowing myself much more than I did ever before. I can relate with myself and can understand with greater compassion how to relate with others. That itself is very powerful.

I say this sincerely. I now feel I have more potential, almost boundless potential, which gives me child-like hope and courage to be free and to get out of the entanglement of fear.

I see the same for you. So here's my encouragement.

Reflect on the original design of you.

Reflect on the feeling of a moment, the fact that you put something great together in this life.

Even if it feels like it's just held together with Scotch tape and bubble gum sometimes, you've gotten yourself to the place where all of the mechanics came together to work for something great. Even if it's just a moment here and there, like me jumping off the second floor with my Scotch tape parachute at age seven.

There is something to rejoice about in that moment, so embrace it, as I did. I do not think I heard a word my mom said when she was scolding me, I was just happy I had done it.

I was excited that it worked. And look, it was such an important moment in my life that it ended up in my book! We are all going to fail. Inevitably, there is some potential for failure in everything we may take on, but enjoy the fact that you tried, that it may have worked to a degree, and enjoy what you learned. You can try again with a little bit more understanding each time.

After falling, I laid there and smiled, knowing (even though my mother saw it as a failure) it had worked to a degree. I thought that now I could try something else to make it even better. I fell, sure, but it was not as bad as I thought it would be. Let's try again and keep on trying.

With eyes wide open and an unyielding heart, embrace the future fearlessly.

We have to acknowledge our inner wisdom because we do not give it enough credit. We do not stop long enough to appreciate who we have become and where we have come from. When we do, and we reflect on ourselves and our learnings, we have to have some compassion for ourselves. We have to have a level of humor that allows us to laugh about ourselves. We have to carry ourselves forward with greater curiosity and compassion.

I think these elements help us respect who we are and also to respect each other.

There is an element of defiance I have had my entire life, which symbolizes a level of courage. It is the human spirit that is common to us all.

With that spirit, there is a triumph that resonates within us: our inner battles, behaviors, and fears share a rhythm of bravery in every one of us.

The introspective realization of my journey, through my career and life, highlights the overcoming of my fears, and not towards a personal victory, but towards hope.

Embracing ourselves and what brings inner peace, joy, calmness, and awareness is a path toward fearlessness and culmination.

It is an ascent toward inspiration and towards hope and courage.

The journey never stops, and there is no end to this story or your own story.

The end is a fallacy.

ENDORSEMENTS

Steve Fowler's Stealth presents an extraordinary journey into the depths of self-discovery and transformation. His stories of navigating cultural identities and confronting his own vulnerabilities offer profound insights into the human psyche and invaluable lessons for anyone seeking self-understanding.

What makes Stealth truly remarkable is Steve's ability to weave universal themes of resilience, adaptability, and growth throughout his anecdotes. Far more than a simple memoir, this book is a guide that inspires and empowers readers to embrace their authentic selves. The thought-provoking and actionable insights Steve offers make it a vital resource for leaders, professionals, and anyone seeking personal growth.

— Dr. Heidi L. D. Marsolek, PhD.

Steve Fowler's Stealth takes a refreshing approach to personal development by challenging readers to confront the illusions and societal pressures keeping them stuck in a cycle of unfulfilling pursuits. Through candid storytelling and introspective insights, Steve encourages readers to embrace their true selves and shed the constraints of societal expectations.

The insights within Stealth remind us that true success comes not from chasing external validation, but from aligning our actions with our core values. The book offers actionable strategies and thought-provoking reflections sure to help readers break free from self-imposed limitations and embrace a life of purpose, courage, and integrity.

— Todd Baxter, Senior Real Estate Executive and Mentor

As a professional who values continuous personal growth, I recommend Stealth to anyone seeking to understand themselves better and achieve greater fulfillment. By blending his rich personal experiences with actionable wisdom, Steve Fowler provides a relatable and encouraging narrative whose essence captures the resilience and adaptability I strive for in my career.

Steve's honesty about his struggles and triumphs offers encouragement for anyone feeling stuck, whether personally or professionally. The valuable lessons on authenticity, leadership, and the power of self-awareness he weaves throughout the book make Stealth a must-read for leaders, professionals, and anyone on a path to growth.

— Kara Matthew, Technology Executive

ABOUT THE AUTHOR

Steve Fowler is a speaker, insightful advisor, and innovative technology executive whose broad experience spans major technology and media landscapes.

As a seasoned leader in these fast-paced industries, Steve has cultivated a deep understanding of diverse team dynamics, leadership strategies, and the nuances of interpersonal communications. His journey through the echelons of corporate leadership has not only afforded him a unique perspective on organizational behavior but also fostered a profound self-discovery, revealing his intrinsic motivations and identity.

Beyond the profession, Steve is an admirer of the arts and a true renaissance man. Though he regrets the loss of his first handmade kerosene-can guitar, a testament to his ingenuity and passion for music, he continues to find solace and joy in strumming the strings of his collection of guitars. His adventurous spirit is also reflected in his love for motorcycle riding and his desire to be an aspiring pilot. This pursuit offers him freedom and a connection with the open road and sky.

Steve's most cherished moments, however, are those spent in the company of his family and friends. Residing near the serene backdrop of Seattle, Washington, a balance of professional achievement, creative expression, and friendships encapsulates the essence of Steve Fowler's life, illustrating a harmonious blend of success, passion, and personal fulfillment.